Toward Improving Canada's Skilled Immigration Policy:

An Evaluation Approach

Charles M. Beach,
Alan G. Green, and
Christopher Worswick

D1367597

Policy Study 45
C.D. Howe Institute

C.D. Howe Institute, 67 Yonge Street,
  Suite 300, Toronto, Ontario M5E 1J8
Phone: (416) 865 1904; Fax: (416) 865 1866;
Internet: www.cdhowe.org

This book is printed on recycled, acid-free paper.

(Policy Study 45)
Includes bibliographical references.
ISBN 978-0-88806-852-1

Printed in Canada by Ricoh, 205 Industrial Parkway North,
  Aurora ON L4G 4C4
October 2011.

W̱e dedicate this study to Professor Alan G. Green, our colleague, mentor, and long-time friend, who unfortunately passed away in November 2010. Alan's gentle wisdom and broad knowledge and insights on Canadian immigration policy will be sorely missed.

Charles Beach
Christopher Worswick

TransCanada
In business to deliver

TransCanada is
pleased to present
you with this 2011/12
shortlisted book

The DONNER Prize

Le Prix DONNER

Contents

Figures

Tables

Foreword

Immigration has been central in Canada's economic, social and cultural development for centuries. Immigration policy deserves, and gets, correspondingly high attention. In recent years, observers and commentators on immigration have highlighted an ominous trend: the gap between earnings of new arrivals in Canada and their Canadian-born contemporaries has been growing, and the time it takes to close that gap has been lengthening. Since 2008, a recession and sluggish recovery accompanied by record numbers of immigrants have made concerns about their impact on the labour market more acute. This study by Charles Beach, Alan Green and Christopher Worswick on the factors underlying immigrants' performance in the workforce, and how Canada might modify its policies to foster better results, is therefore extraordinarily timely.

The focus of Professors Beach, Green and Worswick's work is the number of newcomers admitted under various immigration programs and the way Canada screens potential arrivals from abroad: in particular, the points system used to evaluate the suitability of economic-class immigrants. The balance among arrivals in each category and program, and the weight the points system gives to factors such as age, education, work experience and language skills, are potentially important in explaining the performance of immigrants as a whole in the Canadian labour market. To the extent the evidence suggests they do matter, policymakers can adjust them to improve the likelihood that a typical immigrant will find a good job, that immigrants as a whole will fare better in the workforce, and that the net impact of immigration on Canada's economy will improve.

Readers of this book will find an immense amount of enlightening information in it. Beach, Green and Worswick provide a thorough and expert account of the history of Canadian immigration, the evolution of the policy framework and the points system, and the evidence on immigrants' performance in the workforce. They then proceed to a careful analysis of the correlations between various characteristics of immigrants captured in the points system and the earnings of immigrants upon arrival to Canada. These correlations allow them to simulate how changes in the weights the points system gives to each characteristic might affect entry-level earnings. Those results, combined with their thoughtful consideration of how the various programs and characteristics interact, lead them to several concrete suggestions for changes in the numbers admitted under various programs — giving priority to economic-class immigrants, for example — and for changes in the points system to give greater weights to characteristics such as higher education and job-related language fluency that are clearly correlated with success in the workforce.

Economic criteria such as high entry-level earnings are not and should not be the only factors guiding immigration policy. For both immigrants themselves, and to ensure that immigration continues to be — and is seen as being — beneficial to the country, however, economic consequences matter a lot. Beach, Green and Worswick have given us a thoughtful, readable and constructive analysis of Canadian immigration policy and some practical tools to improve it. This study deserves wide reading among all who are concerned with Canada's economic future and the positive contribution immigrants can make.

In addition to the outstanding work of the authors, it is a pleasure to acknowledge other contributions: a large number of reviewers who provided their own evidence, analysis and suggestions, Colin Busby from the C.D. Howe Institute research team who coordinated the project, Barry Norris and James Fleming who edited the manuscript, and Yang Zhao who prepared it for publication. The analysis and opinions presented in this book are the responsibility of its authors, and do not necessarily represent the views of the C.D. Howe Institute's staff, supporters, or Board of Directors, but I am confident that everyone associated with the Institute will agree that it is a solid contribution to our understanding of a vital policy area.

In acknowledging the talents and accomplishments of the contributors to this book, one sad duty remains: to relate that one of the authors, Alan Green, did not survive to see its publication. I know his colleagues, friends and family will be proud to see this latest top-quality contribution from a devoted scholar who had already made so many. It is a fitting capstone to an outstanding career.

William Robson
President and CEO

Preface and Acknowledgements

This study originated as a follow-on from an earlier piece by the authors, Beach, Green and Worswick (2008), which, in turn, resulted from an invitation by Professor Barry Chiswick to participate in a conference in Chicago on immigration policy in the United States and what that country could learn from the Canadian experience. As two of the distinctive features of Canadian immigration policy since 1967 have been the role of a points system for evaluating prospective economic class immigrants and an important emphasis on skills as a major component of federal immigration policy, we chose to focus on these and ask what effects these features indeed are having on the skills profile of arriving immigrants. This volume extends that line of inquiry by suggesting an objective criterion for judging how skilled immigrants are doing shortly after landing in Canada by looking at what they are earning in the Canadian labour market.

We would thus like to thank — without attributing any errors or shortcomings on the authors' part — Barry Chiswick for sparking our interest in this topic; William Robson at the C.D. Howe Institute for approaching us to undertake this follow-up study; Finn Poschmann, also at the C.D. Howe Institute, for suggesting improvements and a broader focus for the study; and Colin Busby, Ana Ferrer, David Gray, Gilles Grenier, Craig Riddell, and three anonymous referees for their very thoughtful and detailed comments on an earlier draft of this study.

Introduction

The federal government's approach to immigration and the general international context of immigration have faced major challenges in recent years. Accordingly, this is an appropriate time to examine the operations and effectiveness of Canada's policies concerning the inflow of skilled immigrants. Media concerns have highlighted the worsening process of integrating newcomers to the Canadian economy, the large costs of forgone opportunities from not making full use of immigrants' skills, and the complexity and lack of transparency of the current system (see, for example, Paperny 2010; Wente 2010). The media have also raised questions about the type of newcomers Canada should attract and what characteristics likely would lead to immigrants' success in this country (Mahoney 2010). These concerns come at a time when Citizenship and Immigration Canada has announced that, in 2010, Canada landed the largest number of new permanent residents in 50 years (Citizenship and Immigration Canada 2011). This year is also the 60th anniversary of Mabel Timlin's famous treatise, "Does Canada Need More People?" (1951) and the 20th anniversary of the former Economic Council of Canada's influential study on the "Economic and Social Impacts of Immigration" (1991), which first proposed a target rate for immigration of 1 percent of the population.

In terms of Canada's domestic environment, demographic and labour market conditions have dramatically changed since the 1990s. Canada's population and workforce are aging rapidly as birth rates remain below replacement levels, to the extent that immigration soon will account for virtually all Canada's labour force growth. Moreover, the eldest members of the babyboom generation are now reaching retirement age, and the resulting flood of retirees will lead to significant skills shortages that immigration will have to help alleviate.

At the same time, a 15-year period of economic expansion, which led to the tightest labour market in three decades and a shortage of skilled workers, gave way in 2008 to one of the worst recessions since the 1930s and sharply higher unemployment. In such a recessionary labour market, recent immigrants experience far higher rates of unemployment and underemployment than do non-immigrants. As well, the high Canadian dollar and ongoing globalization have led to a marked decline in the manufacturing sector, a traditional source of jobs for immigrants for many decades. There is also an ongoing shift toward a more complex, knowledge-based, skills-oriented economy, and the restarting of employment growth in manufacturing in 2010 has been concentrated in high-technology, high-value-added areas in which immigrants increasingly will have to fit. Many immigrants also must seek employment in the services sector, which traditionally is characterized by relatively lower average earnings levels than in manufacturing. A higher degree of earnings inequality likely will make it harder for immigrants to become integrated fully into the Canadian economy.

Indeed, the past two and a half decades have seen a marked worsening in the adjustment process of new immigrants as their earnings levels have dropped significantly relative to Canadian-born workers, the earnings gap between Canadian- and foreign-born workers has widened, and the catch-up interval between the earnings of immigrants and Canadian-born workers has lengthened. These results have come at the cost of fewer human resources and skills available to the Canadian economy, a potential threat to social cohesion, and the likely loss of skilled immigrants who choose to return home or move on to another country that they see as offering greater opportunities to get ahead.

The international environment for immigration has also been changing rapidly. Growing globalization and, until 2008, years of sustained economic growth in many parts of the world have led to growing international competition for skilled labour. The European Union, for example, recently introduced a "blue card" plan similar to the US green card program to attract skilled labour. A number of other countries, such as the United Kingdom, have recently adopted a point system as part of their effort to attract more skilled labour or are considering such a move (Spain, France, and Denmark). Germany has just announced an effort to attract highly skilled immigrants. Although Canada essentially invented the point system as a keystone of its immigration policy in 1967, that system no longer seem to operate as effectively as it does in, say, Australia, and long delays in the acceptance of immigrants' applications typically occur. And the elephant in the room is the United States, which is now considering bringing in a point system of its own as part of a prospective major restructuring of its immigration policy.

Canada thus needs to respond nimbly to growing international competition for skilled labour or risk falling behind. Workers, particularly skilled workers, are becoming much more internationally mobile as economic opportunities change. The recent financial shock and severe economic recession in many developed economies offer a unique opportunity for Canada to attract skilled young immigrants from these areas. To do so, however, Canada needs to maintain its attractiveness and to replace the lengthy backlogs, complexity, and uncertainty in the current immigration process with a more effective, efficient, and transparent set of procedures.

Recent legislative changes and program developments in the immigration area highlight the need to re-examine the role and effectiveness of Canada's immigration system. In the past several years, the Temporary Foreign Worker Program, which admits largely less-skilled workers, has grown dramatically: between 2006 and 2010, more workers arrived under this program than under the regular Federal Skilled Worker Program, and indeed in 2010 the number exceeded that for all new immigrant arrivals together (Citizenship and Immigration Canada, 2011). This program sought to fill immediate labour market shortages that arose during the long period of economic expansion, especially in the western provinces, but does it make sense to continue the program in an era of relatively high unemployment? Perhaps there is now a need to re-examine the objectives of Canadian immigration policy and its shift to a more short-run, employer-driven economic emphasis. The 2008 Bill C-50, which revised the federal *Immigration and Refugee Protection Act*, also sought to reduce the backlog and speed up the processing of applications, particularly of skilled workers, and delegated substantial additional powers to the Minister of Citizenship and Immigration in pursuit of this aim. It is, however, unclear how these powers will be exercised and what effects they will have on the whole process. Ottawa also implemented a Canadian Experience Class program that makes it easier for foreign students enrolled in post-secondary programs and some temporary foreign workers already working in Canada to apply for permanent immigrant status. In addition, in 2008, Citizenship and Immigration Canada began to require skills-evaluated immigrants to fall into a set of specified occupations listed by the minister, thus shifting immigration policy more toward filling occupational gaps, a role it had played in the 1970s.

These major shifts in recent Canadian immigration policy and practices clearly show the change in the role immigration is viewed as serving. As a result, a tool or criterion now seems to be needed to evaluate how well different classes of immigrants are doing in the Canadian labour market. The purpose of the study, therefore, is to develop such a tool and apply it to an examination of how major policy levers relevant to Canada's skilled worker immigration program affect the earnings levels of workers shortly after their arrival in this country. In developing a useful empirical framework for such an analysis, we provide an extensive survey of recent Canadian literature on immigrant earnings and outcomes. We also critically review recent changes to Canadian immigration policy in light of our criterion, and consider some alternative ways to address current immigration concerns.

The volume proceeds as follows. In Chapter 2, we present a brief history of Canada's immigration system, with a focus on skilled immigration and the point system, and offer an overview of the current structure and operation of the system. In Chapter 3, we review the evidence on major changes in the patterns of immigrants and foreign workers arriving in Canada. Together, these two chapters provide the necessary background material for the volume's core analytical contribution, presented in Chapters 4, 5, and 6. In Chapter 4, we summarize the findings of our recent study of the effects of the point system and major immigration policy levers on the skills characteristics of new arrivals. Then, in Chapter 5, we examine the implications of these results for the development of a tool with which to evaluate how newcomers are doing in the Canadian labour market, as well as the effects of immigrants' skills characteristics on their labour market earnings. In Chapter 6, we present the results of simulating several policy alternatives using an integration of the findings in the previous two chapters. Finally, in Chapter 7, we consider where Canada ought to go from here, and suggest some alternative proposals for reforming Canada's system for the immigration of skilled workers.

Chapter 2

The Development of Canadian Immigration Policy

Immigration has played and continues to play a number of important roles in Canada's development, and different immigration goals have been emphasized at different times in Canada's history (see Green, 1976, 1995, 2003; Green and Green 1999). While a number of distinct goals can be identified, they obviously are overlapping and interconnected. And although we do not mean to diminish immigration's valid and important non-economic roles, our focus is on immigration policy with respect to skilled workers, and so we emphasize the economic role of immigration.

One role of immigration may be referred to simply as nation building (Reitz 2004). Waves of immigrants helped to open the West; provided the manpower to help develop Canada's national resources and build up its manufacturing base, particularly after World War Two; brought energy, skills, and international experience and perspectives to a relatively small country (in terms of population); and helped to mould a perspective of fairness, openness, opportunity, and respect. This led to the growth of a multicultural society, and to the growth and vibrancy of Canada's cities, which are now among the most ethnically and culturally diverse in the world. Indeed, diversity, in its many dimensions, including multiculturalism, has been cited as a distinct social goal of Canada as a nation (Siemiatycki 2005).

Another role of immigration is to contribute to family welfare by facilitating family unification and the sponsoring of relatives to help build the Canadian fabric. This role also has a humanitarian component that brings in a significant number of refugees each year, and thus provides an opportunity to assist many persecuted and unfortunate people from elsewhere in the world (Dolan and Young 2002). Indeed, the 1978 *Immigration Act* identifies three main goals of Canadian immigration policy: to facilitate reunion with close family members, to fulfill Canada's humanitarian refugee commitments, and to foster economic development in all regions of Canada (see Green and Green 1999).

A third role of immigration is to contribute to the demographic growth of Canada (see Health and Welfare Canada 1989; Guillemette and Robson 2006; Banerjee and Robson 2009). This was a primary focus of immigration policy in the later 1980s. Since fertility rates in Canada are below replacement levels, the country's population eventually would peak and then decline were it not for the sizable inflow each year of new arrivals. And since immigrants typically arrive when they are relatively young, they contribute to attenuating the natural aging of the Canadian population, an important consideration now that the large baby boom generation is progressing into its retirement years. Indeed, immigration is a major reason Canada, Australia, and the United States are not aging nearly as rapidly as countries such as Japan, Italy, and Germany, for example, and within 20 years, immigration may account for all of Canada's population growth (Gilmore 2008). A younger workforce is more flexible and adaptable and acquires skills at a faster rate than an older workforce. A 1994 policy statement emphasizes that the "proposed changes [in immigration policy] seek to improve the skills, flexibility and diversity of the Canadian workforce responding to Canada's new emerging economy" (Citizenship and Immigration Canada 1994 p.2). Immigration also offers fiscal benefits to government coffers, since immigrants typically arrive early in their working lives and thus contribute to tax revenues for most of their careers, thus helping to support the baby boom generation in its retirement (Akbari 1989; Smith and Edmonston 1997). Moreover, when elderly babyboomers eventually require home care, immigrants may well be a source of workers to help supply such care.

A fourth role of immigration is the many economic benefits it brings (Borjas 1999; Conference Board of Canada 2009, 2010; Drummond 2009). Immigrants contribute labour market skills that can increase productivity and fill labour market gaps, help maintain economic growth through increasing aggregate expenditure, and facilitate global networks of people and ideas (Peri and Requena-Silvente 2010). Considered in more detail, the economic goals and benefits from immigration can be viewed as both long and short term (Hawkins 1972).

We turn first to long-term arguments for immigration. Studin (2010) argues that a substantially larger population — he suggests a target of 100 million — and economy would greatly increase the talent pool, size of domestic resources, and internal energy of Canadian society, which, in turn, would enhance Canada's strategic power and help shape international outcomes to its advantage. Historically, until World War One, attracting a greater population was an explicit objective to help open up the Canadian West and grow Canada's agricultural sector. Then, in the 1950s, immigration helped to foster the expansion of Canada's primary and manufacturing sectors — some of the current generation of Canada's leading industrialists and entrepreneurs arrived during this period. Simon (1989) argues that a larger labour force increases the potential for innovation and enhanced technological change. Immigration also can be used to generate investment and capital by attracting business class investors, and can serve as a route to increasing international networks and expanding trade flows. Furthermore, increased immigration and a larger economy are said to provide greater opportunities for economies of scale and, hence, increased returns to scale, although evidence for such effects at the national level is not easy to come by, as Canada already had considerable scope for returns to scale in the period following the implementation of the North American Free Trade Agreement. Indeed, as Little (2010) suggests, an important question that no one has answered adequately is "how many immigrants Canada can absorb without leaving some newcomers in economic hardship due to challenges of integrating into a new country?" (Little, 2010 p.2).

A further long-term objective of immigration could be to raise the living standards, or gross domestic product per capita, of current Canadian residents (Drummond and Fong 2010). Again, this could be achieved by enhancing business and technology networks so that Canadian producers have access to the most recent technologies and, indeed, can contribute to developing new ones. Raising living standards could also attract the human capital and skills that would enhance the growth of Canada's modern, knowledge-based economy, an objective of Canadian immigration policy in the 1960s and again since the 1990s. Estimates of the actual effects of immigration on productivity and living standards of incumbent residents, however, are currently a matter of hot debate in the research literature and depend very much on how one characterizes the interactions between immigrants and non-immigrants in the economy's production processes.

Immigration also plays a long-term role in terms of promoting regional economic growth. Canada's regions have different labour force needs that reflect their different resource endowments and historical development, as well as their wish to build local specializations. Programs involving employers and provincial nominees, as well as federal immigration funding agreements with separate provinces, seek to address these more local needs. Proposals have also been made to steer immigrants away from the main magnets of Toronto, Montreal, and Vancouver to smaller urban centres and lower-income regions so as to raise their economic growth rates and help narrow regional income differences (Green 2003). So long as there is freedom of movement within

Canada, however, such proposals may not be very successful, as immigrants generally move to areas where job opportunities are most available.

Turning next to short-term economic roles, immigration is said to bring increased flexibility to the workforce in the sense that immigrants tend to be more geographically mobile than non-immigrants, at least in their initial years in Canada, and to move toward expanding sectors and away from declining ones, thus helping to provide the grease for adjustment as development occurs. Green (1999) also finds that recent immigrants demonstrate greater occupational mobility than do non-immigrants, suggesting that they respond to economic shocks more flexibly than does the native-born workforce.

Finally, immigrants (and temporary foreign workers) help fill immediate occupational gaps and specific skills shortages that cannot be otherwise readily met – for example, seasonal peaks in employment needs in sectors such as agriculture or filling undesirable jobs that Canadian-born workers choose not to do at the going wages. Such employment flexibility on the part of immigrants is also a way for employers to reduce bottlenecks in production processes more quickly and more cost effectively than training Canadian workers to the tasks. This perspective was a major objective of Canadian immigration policy in the 1970s and quite recently has become so again. An aspect of this policy of gap filling writ large is to base the level of immigrant admissions on the so-called absorptive capacity of the Canadian labour market and to use a "tap-on/tap-off" approach to immigration. That is, when the economy is expanding and labour markets are tight, the total number of immigrants admitted should be increased or kept at a relatively high level. But when an economic recession hits, unemployment rates rise, and there is a lot of underutilized domestic labour, the number of immigrant landings should be reduced. This was long a role of immigration until the early 1990s, although total inflow levels have remained relatively stable since then.

Lest the reader be concerned that our discussion of the rationales for immigration appear too positive and one sided, we should note that immigration, like any government policy, has costs as well as benefits. There are fiscal costs to government treasuries of program expenditures directly related to immigration, and social security and transfer expenses related to health, pensions, and income assistance (where entitled) that must be set against the gains from additional tax revenues, in both the short and long run. There are additional congestion costs related to education, training, housing, and urban transit, many of which are borne principally by provincial and local authorities and their taxpayers. And, finally, there are possible economic costs to Canadian residents related to increased inflows of new workers that keep down wages relative to what they would have been in the absence of such additional supply; to reduced job vacancies otherwise available to Canadian workers

— particularly when one breaks down these opportunities by skill groups, industries, and region of residence; and to increased demand for housing and other goods whose prices may be pushed up by the growing population of new arrivals.

An Overview of Early Immigration Policy

The main break between old and new immigration policy in Canada came in 1962, when the federal government abandoned its previously discriminatory approach to immigration, under which the world was divided between preferred and non-preferred countries. In its place, Ottawa adopted a non-discriminatory policy whereby admission would be based on the personal attributes of the individual applicant rather than on his or her place of birth. The concentration in the 1960s on ending discrimination in general was based on two sets of events. First, with the adoption of legislation eliminating discrimination in the workplace, the federal government could hardly continue to permit it to dominate immigration admission practices. Second, Canada in the 1960s was entering a new phase in its economic development, moving from a resource-based economy to an urban industrial economy. This shift required a more sophisticated labour force, and it required it in a hurry, forcing the immigration authorities to search for suitable skilled workers from every corner of the world.

The other major change to Canadian immigration policy in the 1960s was the introduction, in 1967, of the point system, which was meant to insure that the immigration process was equitable for all prospective immigrants regardless of their place of birth. Between the adoption of a universal immigration policy and the introduction of the point system interview, immigration officers felt uncomfortable in judging who was and who was not to be admitted, since the main criterion was now skills, not the more objective one based solely on place of birth. The point system also allowed for the shift of discretionary powers on admission from the minister to the interviewing officer by assigning points or weights to a series of categories and assessing eligibility for admission on the outcome of the sum of the points or test score. The approach was meant to be as transparent and objective as possible, so that decisions by the interviewing officers could be reasonably straightforward.

The end of discrimination among prospective immigrants and the adoption of the point system had a profound effect on the level and composition of immigration to Canada. It is worth noting at this point that, although the system governing admission changed dramatically, one major element of immigration policy remained — namely, the use of the tap-on/tap-off concept that tied immigration levels closely to cyclical economic conditions. The focus of immigration policy thus was inherently short run and, as such, was job-vacancy specific. When the absorptive-capacity model was terminated in the early 1990s, Canadian immigration policy then could be described as non-discriminatory, skills based, objective, and short run.

Before we examine the point system in detail, it might be worth mentioning the various classes of immigrants that entered Canada during this period. The first group to be assessed under the point system was the Economic Class — now those arriving under the Federal Skilled Worker Program (FSWP). The other major class of immigrants was the Family Class, admitted on the basis of kinship with relatives already in Canada. Except for distant relatives, this class was not assessed under the point system. Where relatives were assessed, they received bonus points since it was assumed that relatives already in Canada would assist with any problems they might have in integrating into their host environment. Finally, there was the Refugee Class, which was admitted on the basis of meeting the conditions for refugee status.

Table 1 sets out the categories in which prospective skilled-worker applicants in the Economic Class have been assessed under the point system since 1967. It also shows the weight assigned to each category and the passing grade. Recall that the point system is used to review the applications of economic migrants. The first thing to note is the number of changes the point system has gone through over the time it has been in operation. For example, "experience," "labour market balance," and "levels" did not exist as separate categories in 1967, while categories such as "destination" were operational at the start but played no role in the 1990s. This is in sharp contrast to proposed point system legislation in the United States, which would fix both the immigrant categories and their weights for a decade at a time.

The distribution of weights in the point system across skills categories provides an insight into how immigration policy with respect to skilled workers has changed over the past four decades (the weighting scheme shown for 2004 is the one currently in operation). Three such general policy regimes have operated. The first stretched from 1967 to 1985, during which the focus was on demand-driven, short-run policy. The goal was to match job vacancies to the type of immigrants admitted, as part of the overall economic policy approach to micro-manage the economy. This regime proved generally effective, at least until the recession of the late 1970s, when the inflow of highly trained immigrants continued strongly in the face of a deteriorating domestic market for these skills. Would-be immigrants in this case could build up sufficient points under the "years-of-schooling," "age," and "language facility" categories to score over 50 points, thus overriding the fact that there was already a surplus of workers seeking employment in intended occupations.

Table 1: The Canadian Point System since 1967

Factor	1967 (1)	1974 (2)	1978 (3)	1986 (4)	1993 (5)	1996 (6)	2004 (7)
				(maximum points)			
Long-run factors							
Education	20	20	12	12	14	21	25
Experience	/	/	8	8	8	9	21
Age	10	10	10	10	10	13	10
Language	10	10	10	15	14	21	24
Subtotal	**40**	**40**	**40**	**45**	**46**	**64**	**80**
Short-run factors							
Specific vocational preparation	10	10	15	15	16	/	/
Occupational demand	15	15	15	10	10	/	/
Labour market balance	/	/	/	/	/	10	/
Arrange employment or designated occupation	10	10	10	10	10	4	10
Personal suitability or adaptability	15	15	10	10	10	17	10
Levels adjustment factor[a]	/	/	/	10	8	/	/
Relative [b,c]	0/3/5[d]	0/3/5	5	/	/	5	/
Destination	5	5	5	/	/	/	/
Subtotal	**60**	**60**	**60**	**55**	**54**	**36**	**20**
Total	**100**	**100**	**100**	**100**	**100**	**100**	**100**
Pass mark[e]	**50**	**50**	**50**	**70**	**67**	**f**	**67**

Notes:

Maximum points and pass mark have been rescaled for 1993 and 1996 to put the system in terms of points out of 100 throughout the period.

Bars on entry: 1967 — no one category result conclusive either way; February 1974 — applicant must either receive at least one unit for occupational demand or get ten points for arranged employment or a designated occupation; October 1974 — ten points deducted unless the applicant showed evidence of arranged employment or was going to a designated occupation, removed in April 1979 but reimposed in September 1979; May 1982 — only applicants with arranged employment eligible for admission, removed in January 1986; 1992 — zero units for experience an automatic bar unless the person has arranged employment.

[a] A discretionary allocation that can be used to control the number of persons entering over a period.

[b] Relative factor was eliminated as of 1986 as a selection factor for independent/skilled worker applicants.

[c] Regulatory change on January 1, 1986, established a "kinship bonus" for "Assisted Relative" applicants. Before that, such applicants were not assessed on the following factors: arranged employment, language, relative, or destination. The total and pass mark varied under each regime for Assisted Relatives.

[d] Points awarded depend on relationship to sponsor.

[e] The pass mark applied to independent/skilled worker applicants.

[f] The pass mark varies by skill group. The pass marks are: 52 for professionals and skilled administrators, 47 for technical workers, and 45 for trades; total available points actually equal 74.

This gap-filling approach can be seen in Table 1. Until the mid-1980s, short-run factors dominated the distribution of points, accounting for around two-thirds of the total points needed to gain admission as a skilled worker and professional immigrant. The major change during this period was the requirement that would-be immigrants score at least one point under "arranged employment" before being granted admission. Among the long-run points, the major change was the decline in the weight given to "education," which fell from a maximum of 20 points in 1967 to 12 points in 1978. At the same time, "specific vocational preparation" (on-the-job training) increased in weight from 10 to 15 points.

The passage of the 1978 *Immigration Act* was partly in response to problems with the gap-filling approach. The act changed the central element of Canadian immigration policy by shifting processing priority to family reunification and refugee applicants ahead of economic immigrants. As a result, the share of economic immigrants declined as this group became the residual class of those to be admitted. However, the short-run, or absorptive-capacity, approach to setting the level of immigration continued to operate during this period.

The second period of evolution of the skilled worker system, which stretched from the mid-1980s to the mid-1990s, bridges the first and third periods under review. The main focus during those years was on demographic concerns, rather than on economic factors. Federal government studies suggested that Canada's low fertility rates implied the long-run aging of the population. One solution would have been to increase levels of immigration, but it quickly became evident that, if immigration was to lower the average age of the population significantly, inflows would have to be much higher than was politically acceptable. Nevertheless, the debate over the role of immigration to solve this demographic concern represented a victory of sorts for those who saw immigration policy directed toward long-run, rather than short-run, factors.

In line with this shift in thinking about the role of immigration went the position that skilled or economic immigrants would continue to be the residual class, and that the focus should remain on family reunification or humanitarian ends. Such a shift meant that the share of immigrants admitted under the point system remained low — about 30 percent of the total — the net result of which was to lower the average skills level of those landing in Canada. It is worth mentioning at this point that, over this period and continuing into the next, the level of immigration increased sharply and its geographic source distribution shifted toward Asian and Latin American countries and away from traditional sources of immigration – as we examine in more detail later in the study.

The third period of evolution of the skilled worker system, which operated from 1993 to the first quarter of 2008, witnessed changes in immigration policy that rivalled those of the 1960s. First, immigration policy shifted toward economic immigrants and away from both a family reunification and a humanitarian focus. The goal was to have the division about equal in numbers between economic and non-economic immigrants. In a way, the sharpened focus on economic immigrants was a return to the traditional stance of immigration as part of overall economic policy. Second, believing that Canada could not compete adequately for skilled immigrants using a short-run policy stance, Ottawa shifted immigration policy toward a long-run orientation by abandoning the absorptive-capacity, or tap-on/tap-off, approach that had been the hallmark of immigration policy since the early 1900s. In its place, the federal government instituted a 1 percent (or slightly less) annual inflow target that did not change with short-run changes in unemployment levels.

Finally, as Table 1 shows, in the third period, the point scores themselves shifted toward the long-run factors of "education" and "experience," increasing the share of long-run factors in the total to 64 percent by 1996 and to 80 percent by 2004. As a result, by the turn of the twenty-first century, Canadian immigration policy had become non-discriminatory, long run, and focused on building human capital in the labour force. Later in this study, we examine how recent revisions to the *Immigration and Refugee Protection Act* have again altered this structure of immigration policy.

It is useful to keep in mind that what are referred to generally as economic class immigrants currently consist of a number of distinct categories (the numbers that follow are from Citizenship and Immigration Canada 2011). The largest component is skilled worker principal applicants under the FSWP, of which there were 48,815 in 2010 (along with their spouses and dependants — 70,524 in 2010). Only these applicants are skills-assessed under the point system. Together, the number of permanent residents landing under this program was just over 119,000 in 2010 out of a total of Economic Class landings of nearly 187,000, or about 66 percent of all such immigrants. Landings under the entrepreneur and self-employed categories were just 1,586 in 2010, while those coming in under the investors program numbered 11,715, and under the live-in caregivers program, 13,906. The Provincial Nominee Programs (PNP) brought in a further 36,419 in 2010, and the new Canadian Experience Class category accounted for 3,916 landings.

Recent Changes to Immigration Programs

Although a number of changes have been made to Canada's immigration program, it is important to note that two key components have not changed.

First, Canada's Constitution gives the federal and provincial governments concurrent jurisdiction over immigration. This is reflected, for example, in Citizenship and Immigration Canada's regular consulting processes with the provinces to set projected annual target ranges for the total inflow of immigrants and for its major components, and to enter into agreements with individual provinces on various aspects of immigration and settlement policy. An example of the latter is the Canada-Quebec Accord of 1991, under which Quebec sets its own immigration levels and selects skilled workers under its own point system for immigrants arriving in that province (Dolin and Young 2002, 14). Second, the federal government — as in the last major economic recession of the early 1990s — has maintained total immigration levels more or less at pre-recession levels, rather than cutting back on admissions, which it traditionally followed in previous recessions and which countries such as Australia and the United Kingdom continue to do. Indeed, as we discuss later, the number of temporary foreign workers and provincial nominee admissions actually has increased.

Notwithstanding these continuing aspects of Canada's immigration program, there have been four major sets of changes with respect to the skilled immigration process: (i) the introduction of the *Immigration and Refugee Protection Act* (IRPA) and the issuance of ministerial instructions related to the processing of applications under the FSWP; (ii) the enhanced role of temporary foreign workers; (iii) the increased role of the PNP; and (iv) the introduction of the Canadian Experience Class of immigrants.

In April 2008, the federal government introduced new immigration legislation, as part of Bill C-50, which subsequently became part of the IRPA, under which Citizenship and Immigration Canada essentially operates. These amendments to the IRPA came into force immediately, and applications for admission made on or since February 27, 2008, have come under the new regulations. The changes to the IRPA plot a new direction for immigration policy (the so-called Action Plan for Faster Immigration) and were made to address two immediate problems and a third, longer-run problem: (i) to eliminate the backlog of as many as a million application files; (ii) to create a set of regulations that would be more responsive to immediate labour market needs in what then was viewed as an era of labour shortages, a sustained economic expansion, and historically low unemployment rates; and (iii) declining immigrant outcomes in the Canadian labour market.

First, under the new arrangements, the minister can give instructions concerning the processing of applications "in a manner that, in the opinion of the Minister, will best support the attainment of the immigration goals established by the Government of Canada" (sect. 87.3(2) of the amended act), establish "an order...for the processing of applications" (sect. 87.3(3b)), set "the number of applications or requests...to be processed in any year" (sect. 87.3(3c)), and provide "for the dispositions of applications and requests" (sect. 87.3(3d)). Consequently, the minister could simply return an unprocessed application (with the fee), approve the application for admission, or possibly hold the application for future reference.

In addition, between November 27, 2008, and June 36, 2010, ministerial instructions were issued as part of the Action Plan for Faster Immigration to make the FSWP more responsive to labour market needs, partly by introducing new criteria for applications under the program and with the goal of reducing wait times for the processing of applications to between six and twelve months. Now, to be rush processed, applicants must: (i) already have an offer of arranged employment; (ii) have experience working in any of 38 specified in-demand occupations (subsequently reduced to 29); or (iii) be either a temporary foreign worker or a student residing in Canada for at least one year. Applications by people falling into at least one of these three categories are to be fast tracked, while the rest are rejected and the applicant's fee is refunded. Since some of the specified occupations require credentials and qualifications, in November 2009 the federal government signed an agreement with the provinces and territories to work, over the next three years, to address barriers to the recognition of those earned abroad.

These ministerial instructions represent a significant change from previous regulations that required Citizenship and Immigration Canada to process all applications to a final decision. Now, the minister can cherry pick applicants who match the department's occupational priority list, thus saving resources in the selection of immigrants, and seek to match the supply of foreign workers to current demand for their skills. While this process raises the possibility of some form of pre-screening based on criteria that could be less than transparent or even discriminatory, it should be noted that section 3 of the IRPA holds that anything the department does must comply with the Charter of Rights and Freedoms.

To be clear, the ministerial instructions do not remove the need for an FSWP applicant to be assessed against the point grid. Rather, they operate as a front-end filter. In addition, the instructions apply the occupation list only to applications under the FSWP and do not affect applications in any other category. It is also worth noting that, until the FSWP backlog is eliminated, the majority of annual admissions in this category will still be those who applied prior to the introduction of the ministerial instructions.

The second major change in recent policy toward skilled foreign workers in Canada is the much enhanced role now played by temporary foreign workers (see Sweetman and Warman 2010a; Worswick 2010a). Such workers are intended to address short-term national or regional shortages of specific skills or labour needs. To bring in a temporary foreign worker for a specified job and period of time, an employer must satisfy Human Resources and Skills Development Canada that it has not been able to hire a Canadian or permanent resident for the job. In the past few years, however, the size of the temporary workers program has expanded dramatically, with the number of new entrants rising from 112,600 in 2004 to 182,300 in 2010; in fact, since 2007, the number of incoming temporary foreign workers has exceeded that of Economic Class immigrants (Citizenship and Immigration Canada 2009, 48–49). One reason for the popularity of this program, as noted by Canada's auditor general, is that "[t]he long delays and the criteria used in the processing of applications under the…FSW category also led employers to rely on temporary workers to address their immediate labour needs" (Auditor General of Canada 2009, 28). Indeed, as the auditor general further notes, a pilot project since 2002 for bringing in lower-skilled workers now accounts "for more than half of all temporary foreign workers in Canada" (34).

The third recent major change in policy toward the immigration of skilled workers is a substantial increase in the role of the Provincial Nominee Program. The objectives of this program and of agreements between the federal government and all provinces and one territory are to select immigrants who correspond to various provincial and local labour market needs and hence are more locally responsive, and to attract immigrants to smaller urban areas and regions with only a limited historic immigrant tradition, in accordance with the objective of promoting regional economic growth. Under these federal-provincial agreements, each province chooses its own selection criteria and nominees who satisfy these criteria. Citizenship and Immigration Canada is then committed to process all such nominees for permanent residence as a top priority As the auditor general notes, "Provincial nominees are not subject to the requirements of the point system applicable to the…FSW category, nor does [Citizenship and Immigration Canada] impose any minimum selection threshold for these candidates…At the time of our audit, they included more than 50 different categories, each with its own selection approach and criteria. PNP agreements do not require provinces and territories to obtain [Citizenship and Immigration Canada]'s approval when they create new PNP categories; they are required only to inform [the department]" (Auditor General of Canada 2009, 25).

It is not surprising, then, that immigrant admissions under these programs have also increased dramatically, from 477 in 1999 to 36,419 in 2010 (Citizenship and Immigration Canada 2011). Nominees can be from among current temporary foreign workers, and again this route provides an opportunity for employers to avoid the delays and basic skills requirements in the federal point system in order to address their immediate labour market needs.

The fourth recent major change in policy toward skilled immigration is the establishment in September 2008 of the new Canadian Experience Class. This class targets the two groups of highly skilled temporary foreign workers and foreign post-secondary students already resident in Canada. The rationale is that these people are already functioning successfully within the Canadian environment, are acquiring credentials and actual Canadian work experience that Canadian employers will fully understand and value, and have already had an opportunity to operate in the workplace in English or French and hence are likely reasonably proficient in either language, and can readily integrate into the Canadian labour market. Applicants who are temporary foreign workers must have at least two years of Canadian work experience in a high-skilled occupation. Applicants who have been foreign post-secondary students in Canada must have graduated from a recognized full-time post-secondary program in Canada of at least two years in length and also have one year of Canadian work experience in their chosen field of training. They do not need to leave the country in order to apply, nor do they need to meet the federal point system requirements relevant for regular skilled worker applicants. Applications under this program are fast tracked, but the number is counted within, rather than in addition to, the total target of federal Economic Class immigrants, so there will be a corresponding reduction in the number of skilled workers coming through the regular federal point system route. While it is too early to tell what the take-up rate will be for this program, Citizenship and Immigration Canada estimates that the number of successful applicants will increase from around 5,000 in 2009 to around 26,000 by 2012 (Auditor General of Canada 2009, 28).

Several more specific changes have also been made by ministerial instructions. For example, on March 10, 2010, the federal government announced a streamlining of the process for assessing language skills of FSWP and Canadian Experience Class applicants, who now must provide independent third-party test results of their English-or French-language ability when submitting their application. Previously, applicants initially assessed their own language skills, which could then be revised by the opinion of the visa officer during an interview, resulting in requests for further evidence and processing delays. Assessment is based on being able to speak, read, and write either English or French with difficulty, well, or fluently, with additional points awarded for facility in both languages.

Challenges Facing Skilled Immigration Policy

Some recent changes in Canada's approach to skilled immigration were made in response to a number of major challenges that have been brought into sharper focus by the recent recession and rise in unemployment in Canada and elsewhere, and by the increasing international competition for skilled workers, particularly from Australia, the United Kingdom, and several other western European countries (see Skills Research Initiative 2008). While we examine some of these challenges in more detail later in the volume, it is worthwhile to draw attention to them right from the outset.

The first major challenge is that immigrants who have landed over the past three or more decades have not fared as well in the labour market as Canadian-born workers and have not integrated as readily into the Canadian economy. Canadian employers discount foreign education, training, and work experience, and, as noted above, immigrants typically face difficulties obtaining professional recognition of their foreign credentials and qualifications, which involves not only a waste of the skills of new arrivals but also a loss of human expectations and pride. Of particular concern are rising poverty rates among immigrants and the persistent and worsening earnings gap between immigrants and Canadian-born workers at a time when Canada enjoyed the longest period of economic expansion in decades. The result is underemployment of human resources and the loss of workers who choose to return home or move to a third country (often, the United States) where greater opportunities may be available.

Second, the Canadian point system evaluation screen heavily reflects long-term white-collar skills (such as education and work experience), but fails to take adequate account of the demand side of the labour market, the need for blue-collar and trades skills, and rapid changes in types of skills in demand in the economy. In the early to mid-1990s, when the point system went through its last significant review, the Canadian labour market was vastly different: unemployment was high, production was being restructured to accommodate North American free trade, western energy developments were not nearly as advanced, major government cutbacks and layoffs were occurring at all levels, and the wave of baby boom retirements was still well in the future. All this has now changed, and a major rethink of the Canadian point system to recognize a broader range of skills and to respond to labour shortages and the need for specific skills seems very much in order.

Third, although the federal approach to these challenges has involved reducing target levels for entrants under the FSWP and sharply increasing the number of both temporary foreign workers entering Canada and immigrants coming in under the PNP, this response entails its own problems. Many temporary foreign workers are low skilled, which creates disincentives for employers to retrain unemployed Canadians and move them to where the jobs are, thus inhibiting the price adjustment system in the labour market — employers that become dependent on a continuing supply of foreign workers are less likely to seek out domestic alternatives. Instead, low-skilled foreign workers are brought in, typically on two- or three-year visas, to fill current private sector employment shortages. But when a recession hits or sectoral shifts in demand occur, such workers can be laid off, and who then has responsibility for them? There is thus a difference between private short-run needs and public or social long-run costs and benefits. If temporary foreign workers are laid off, they can stay legally in Canada until their visas expire, but cannot collect employment insurance or social assistance, which gives them an incentive to remain in Canada and take lower-paying jobs with no work security. This fosters the growth of a peripheral workforce that is readily subject to employment abuse. Also, temporary foreign workers are tied to specific employers, which can lead to abuse and exploitation, as such workers do not have the full rights of permanent workers (see Nakache and Kinoshita 2010). The experience of other countries — particularly in western Europe — shows that such programs can lead to social and political problems if these workers choose not to return to their home country once their employment stint ends (Martin 2010). Moreover, as the auditor general notes, there is "a lack of timely program evaluation for the [Temporary Foreign Worker Program]" (Auditor General of Canada 2009, 15).

Under the PNP, private employers typically can nominate suitable prospects – including from among current temporary foreign workers – whom the province then screens for local suitability and passes their names on to the federal authorities for medical and security clearance. Citizenship and Immigration Canada then can fast track such nominees without their having to go through any point system review — that is, they do not need to meet federal (or other minimum) skills requirements. Again, however, the system in effect is making long-run decisions on the basis of short-run perspectives, and it raises what economists call a moral hazard problem in that employers can use this route to bring in workers for their current needs, but job losses among such workers then impose a fiscal burden on the public sector and increased competition for jobs among low-wage workers. Moreover, the various separate agreements between Ottawa and the provinces lead to a patchwork of entrance criteria, which potential applicants abroad may find confusing and which adds to the perceived uncertainty and lack of transparency of the admission process (Alboim and Maytree Foundation 2009).

Fourth, the role of the long-run human capital model that has dominated immigration policy since the early 1990s is diminishing in favour of a shift back to an occupational gap-filling perspective for bringing in immigrant workers. As noted above, the federal government now requires all applicants under the FSWP to fall within a certain number of designated in-demand occupations, which takes policy back to what prevailed in the 1970s and early

1980s. This approach was unsuccessful then (see Green and Green 1999) because occupations are hard to define appropriately, labour market gaps are hard to identify in a timely fashion, and bureaucracy cannot keep up with the quickly evolving needs of the Canadian labour market. It was for precisely these reasons that skilled worker policy shifted toward a point system based on broader skill sets such as education, work experience, language fluency, and the adaptability of youth.

Fifth, despite recent changes, Canada still has a huge backlog of applications under the FSWP — more than 620,000 people were waiting in December 2008 — as well as an average processing period of 63 months for a decision (Auditor General of Canada 2009, 2); in Australia, in contrast, the processing time is about six months. As a result, many applicants become frustrated and either give up, if economic conditions are improving in their home countries, or simply go elsewhere. Again, the auditor general concludes: "Measures taken by [Citizenship and Immigration Canada] in 2008 to limit the number of new applications — for example, processing only those that meet new, more narrowly defined criteria — were not based on sufficient analysis of their potential effects" (Auditor General of Canada 2009, 2).

In light of the recent shift of immigration objectives from a long-run to a more short-run perspective and away from the FSWP to a more occupational gap-filling orientation, it would be useful to find a way to estimate what skilled immigrants bring to the Canadian economy. It is to this principal objective of the study that we now turn.

| Chapter 3 | *Changing Patterns of Immigration to Canada* |

Immigration plays an important role in Canada's demographics and labour force growth. In 2006, for example, there were 6.19 million foreign-born residents in Canada, which represented 19.8 percent of the total population and 21.2 percent of the labour force (Statistics Canada 2008b, 29). Between the two census years 2001 and 2006, the immigrant population went up by 13.6 percent, compared with only 3.3 percent for the Canadian-born population (Statistics Canada 2007, 5), thus accounting for more than two-thirds of Canada's population growth over that period. Indeed, given current demographic trends, immigration shortly will constitute almost all of Canada's population growth.

Table 2 shows how the immigration rate (in terms of annual landings) has varied considerably over the past century. It was extremely high (4.1–5.3 percent of the population per year) in 1910 through 1913 as the prairie provinces were being opened up to settlement just prior to World War One. During the Great Depression and World War Two, the immigration rate fell precipitously to just 0.1–0.3 percent of the population per year. Then, during the 1950s, it climbed to around 1.0 percent of the population per year — rising to 1.7 percent in 1957 when Canada accepted a large number of Hungarian refugees following the failed revolution in that country. Through the 1960s, 1970s, and up to the mid-1980s, the immigration rate averaged considerably less than 1.0 percent of the population per year. Then, from 1986 to 1993, the rate rose steadily from 0.4 percent (99,000 per year) to 0.9 percent (257,000 per year). Since then, except in 1998 and 1999, arrivals have remained above 200,000 per year — reaching as high as 280,600 in 2010 — but still representing less than 1.0 percent of the population per year.

Table 2: Inflow of Immigrants to Canada, 1901–2008

	Number	As percent of Canada's Population		Number	As percent of Canada's Population
	(thousands)	(%)		(thousands)	(%)
1901	55.7	1.0	2000	227.5	0.7
1911	331.3	4.6	2001	250.6	0.8
1921	91.7	1.0	2002	229.0	0.7
1931	27.5	0.3	2003	221.3	0.7
1941	9.3	0.1	2004	235.8	0.7
1951	194.4	1.4	2005	262.2	0.8
1961	71.7	0.4	2006	251.6	0.8
1971	121.9	0.6	2007	236.8	0.7
1981	128.6	0.4	2008	247.2	0.7
1991	232.8	0.8	2009	252.2	0.8
			2010	280.6	0.8

Source: Citizenship and Immigration Canada (2009, 3), and Citizenship and Immigration Canada (2010). The figures for 2010 are preliminary.

Canada's immigration rate, as a percentage of the population, is second only to that of Australia among major immigrant-receiving industrialized countries. As Table 3 shows, while the United States takes in far more immigrants — more than a million in 2005 — than do the other countries listed, immigrants account for a smaller proportion of the population in the United States than in Canada or Australia. Also, since immigrants on average tend to move early in their careers and then work hard to get established in their new land, they constitute a larger fraction of the labour force in their host countries than their share of the total population.

A major feature of Canada's evolving immigration pattern is the quite dramatic change in the source of new immigrants over the past 40 years. As shown in Figure 1, in 1971 the major sources were Europe and the United States. Then during the 1970s, the proportion of immigrants arriving from Europe decreased markedly, while that from Asia and the Middle East more than doubled. By 2006, Asia and the Middle East were far and away the major source regions, while Europe and the United States accounted for only about 20 percent of total immigrants. Table 4 shows this changing pattern for the top ten source countries between 1981 and 2006, with the United Kingdom slipping from first to ninth spot and China moving from tenth to first.

A consequence of this major shift in source countries is the increasing difficulty immigrants face in adjusting — culturally, socially, and economically — to their new environment. An important component of this challenge is language. As Figure 2 shows, the proportion of arriving immigrants with

Table 3: Immigration Inflows and Stocks, Major Receiving Countries, 2005

	Inflow *(thousands)*	Immigrants as percent of Population *(%)*	Inflow as percent of Population *(%)*	Immigrants as percent of Labour Force *(%)*	Stock of Immigration *(millions)*
Australia	180	20.3	0.89	25.7	4.1
Canada	**262**	**18.9**	**0.81**	**21.2**	**6.1**
France	170	10.7	0.28	12.0	6.5
Germany	241	12.3	0.29	n.a.	10.1
Italy	199	4.3	0.34	8.6	2.5
United Kingdom	363	9.1	0.61	11.2	5.4
United States	1,122	12.9	0.38	15.7	38.4

Sources: Columns 1 and 4 from OECD (2008, 29, 69); labour force figures are for 2006. Columns 2 and 5 from World Bank (2008). Columns 3 figures are calculated from columns 1, 2, and 5.

Figure 1: Region of Birth of Recent Immigrants to Canada, 1971–2006

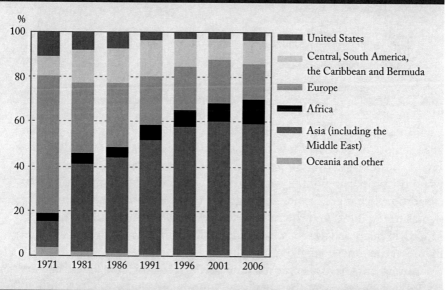

Sources: Statistics Canada (2007, 9).

Table 4: Top Ten Countries of Birth of Immigrants to Canada, 1981–2006

Order	1981 Census	1991 Census	1996 Census	2001 Census	2006 Census
1	United Kingdom	Hong Kong	Hong Kong	China	China
2	Vietnam	Poland	China	India	India
3	United States	China	India	Philippines	Philippines
4	India	India	Philippines	Pakistan	Pakistan
5	Philippines	Philippines	Sri Lanka	Hong Kong	United States
6	Jamaica	United Kingdom	Poland	Iran	South Korea
7	Hong Kong	Vietnam	Taiwan	Taiwan	Romania
8	Portugal	United States	Vietnam	United States	Iran
9	Taiwan	Lebanon	United States	South Korea	United Kingdom
10	China	Portugal	United Kingdom	Sri Lanka	Colombia

Sources: Statistics Canada (2007, 10).

English as their mother tongue has been steadily decreasing since at least 1981, while the proportion with a mother tongue other than English or French has risen to over 80 percent. This change has been occurring at a time when the proportion of the workforce in primary and manufacturing jobs — a traditional channel for new immigrants to get established economically — has been falling, and the role of services in the economy has been rising. Indeed, in many services jobs, especially well-paying professional ones, fluency in one of the official languages is critical.

Immigrants have also settled unevenly across provinces and urban areas. As Table 5 shows, more than half of all immigrants between 2001 and 2006 settled in Ontario, while Quebec received more than 17 percent and British Columbia 16 percent. In terms of the total stock of immigrants as of 2006, 55 percent reside in Ontario, 18 percent in British Columbia, and about

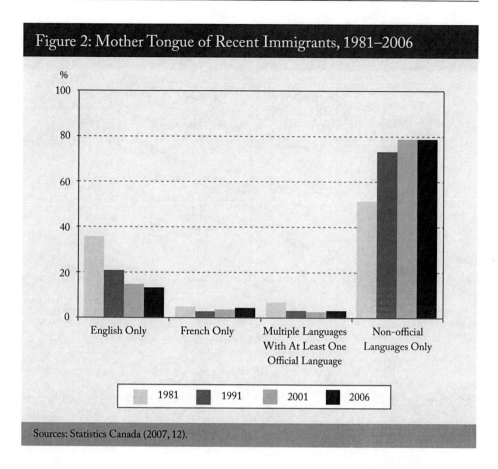

Figure 2: Mother Tongue of Recent Immigrants, 1981–2006

Legend: 1981, 1991, 2001, 2006

Sources: Statistics Canada (2007, 12).

14 percent in Quebec. The prairie provinces attracted about 13 percent of recent immigrants, and only 1.2 percent settled in Atlantic Canada. Immigrants also settle predominantly in the three largest urban areas: as of 2006, 40.4 percent of recent immigrants settled in Toronto, 14.9 percent in Montreal, and 13.7 percent in Vancouver. Another 28 percent went to other urban areas across the country, and only 3 percent ended up living in rural areas. The result is that Toronto, Montreal, and Vancouver have among the highest proportion of immigrants of any large cities in the major immigrant-receiving countries. Indeed, Toronto and Vancouver lead the pack with 46 percent and 40 percent, respectively, foreign-born (see Figure 3). So immigration in Canada is very much an urban phenomenon.

Finally, immigrants tend to arrive in Canada at a young age relative to the average age of all Canadians. Immigrating while one is young provides a longer period in which to gain the benefits relative to the costs of such a major move, and younger people generally adapt faster to a new environment than do older people. For this reason, immigration is often viewed as a way

Table 5: Distribution of Total Population, Total Immigrant Population and Recent Immigrants, Canada and the Provinces, 2006

Place of Residence	Distribution of Total Canadian Population	Distribution of Total Immigrant Population[a]	Distribution of Recent Immigrants[b]
NFLD	1.6	0.1	0.1
PEI	0.4	0.1	0.1
NS	2.9	0.7	0.6
NB	2.3	0.4	0.4
QC	23.8	13.8	17.5
ON	38.5	54.9	52.3
MB	3.6	2.4	2.8
SK	3.1	0.8	0.7
AB	10.4	8.5	9.3
BC	13.0	18.1	16.0
Canada	100.0	100.0	100.0

a The 2006 census defines "immigrant population," also known as "foreign-born population," as persons who are, or have been, landed immigrants in Canada.
b Immigrants who came to Canada between January 1, 2001 and May 16, 2006.
Source: Statistics Canada (2007, 14).

to slow down the aging of Canada's population. Table 6 shows that, while the proportion of recent immigrants in 2006 younger than age 25 was not much different than for the population as a whole, the proportion of prime working age (25 to 54) was 15 percentage points higher and that of the older group (age 55 and older) was about 15 points lower. Immigrants are thus more concentrated in the earnings period of their life cycle, when issues of labour market skills and employability are important.

Immigrant Admission Categories and Temporary Workers

As noted earlier, immigration to Canada serves several goals or objectives: economic, social, and humanitarian among them. The *2002 Immigration and Refugee Protection Act* (IRPA) correspondingly identifies three major categories of admissions: those that contribute to economic development in Canada, those that reunite families, and those that protect refugees. As the act states,

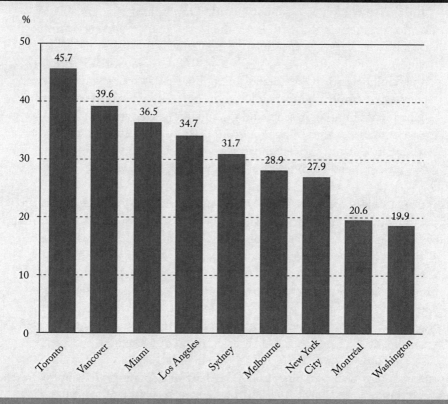

Figure 3: Foreign-born as a Percentage of Metropolitan Population, Selected Cities, 2006

Sources: Statistics Canada (2007, 19).

Table 6: Age Distribution of Recent Immigrants and Total Canadian Population, 2006

Age Group	Recent Immigrants	Total Population
	(percent)	
Under 15	20.1	21.1
15–24	15.1	14.4
25–54	57.3	42.3
55–64	4.1	10.7
65 and older	3.4	11.5
Total	**100.0**	**100.0**

Note: Recent immigrants refer to immigrants who came to Canada between January 1, 2001, and May 16, 2006.
Source: Statistics Canada (2007, 13).

Economic immigrants are people selected for their skills and ability to contribute to Canada's economy, including skilled workers, business immigrants, provincial and territorial nominees and live-in caregivers. The skilled worker component includes immigrants who are able to demonstrate their ability to enter the labour market and successfully establish in Canada by meeting selection criteria that assess factors such as education, English or French language abilities and work experience.... The family class is comprised of foreign nationals sponsored by close relatives or family members in Canada and includes spouses and partners, dependent children, parents and grandparents. Refugees include government-assisted refugees, privately sponsored refugees, refugees landed in Canada and dependants of refugees landed in Canada. (Citizenship and Immigration Canada 2009, 1.)

A fourth admission category — "Other Immigrants" — includes those admitted under discretionary provisions of the act who would not otherwise qualify under the first three categories, as well as residual administrative cases.

The relative sizes of these four admission categories are set out in Table 7. The two largest are the Economic Class and the Family Class. In 1984, immigrants admitted under the former category accounted for less than 30 percent of new arrivals, while those coming in under the latter accounted for about half. Since then, the relative positions of the two classes have reversed. Big run-ups in Economic Class arrivals occurred over the mid-1980s and during the mid- to later 1990s, while the share of Family Class immigrants correspondingly declined. Since 2000, the share of Economic Class immigrants, though jumping up sharply in 2010, has averaged around 60 percent and Family Class admissions have varied between 22 and 28 percent. So there has clearly been a major shift in immigration flows toward an emphasis on skills and the economic role of immigration. The United States, by contrast, has an approach to immigration focused more on family reunification, while the Economic Class proportion of immigrants is higher than in Australia.

The numbers and proportions of refugees vary a lot from year to year depending in part on world events outside Canada. While the numbers of landed refugees in recent years have generally been in the range of 20,000 to 35,000 per year, their share of the total has declined slightly to between 9 and 14 percent. The "Other Immigrants" category typically is quite minor, usually accounting for only 2 to 5 percent of the total.

Canada also has a number of temporary foreign residents, two major categories of which are temporary foreign workers and foreign students studying in Canada. According to Citizenship and Immigration Canada, "Foreign workers are those other than Canadian citizens or permanent

Table 7: Immigrant Landings by Admission Categories, 1984–2008

	Economic Class	Family Class	Refugees	Other Immigrants	Total
	(number; % of total in parentheses)				
1984	26,079 (29.5)	44,521 (50.4)	15,361 (17.4)	2,315 (2.6)	88,276
1985	26,112 (31.0)	39,361 (46.7)	16,772 (19.9)	2,101 (2.5)	84,346
1986	35,839 (36.1)	42,475 (42.8)	19,204 (19.3)	1,835 (1.8)	99,353
1987	74,108 (48.7)	53,840 (35.4)	21,470 (14.1)	2,666 (1.8)	152,084
1988	80,220 (49.6)	51,425 (31.8)	26,765 (16.6)	3,172 (2.0)	161,582
1990	97,933 (45.2)	74,686 (34.5)	40,236 (18.6)	3,601 (1.7)	216,456
1992	95,803 (37.6)	101,122 (39.7)	52,349 (20.5)	5,544 (2.2)	254,818
1994	102,311 (45.6)	94,195 (42.0)	20,436 (9.1)	7,454 (3.3)	224,396
1996	125,370 (55.5)	68,359 (30.2)	28,478 (12.6)	3,865 (1.7)	226,072
1998	97,912 (56.2)	50,896 (29.2)	22,843 (13.1)	2,547 (1.5)	174,198
2000	136,290 (59.9)	60,616 (26.6)	30,092 (13.2)	460 (0.2)	227,458
2002	137,863 (60.2)	62,290 (27.2)	25,116 (11.0)	3,780 (1.7)	229,049
2004	133,748 (56.7)	62,261 (26.4)	32,687 (13.9)	7,129 (3.0)	235,825
2005	156,312 (59.6)	63,361 (24.2)	35,776 (13.6)	6,790 (2.6)	262,239
2006	138,252 (54.9)	70,508 (28.0)	32,499 (12.9)	10,382 (4.1)	251,641
2007	131,244 (55.4)	66,232 (28.0)	27,955 (11.8)	11,322 (4.8)	236,753
2008	149,071 (60.3)	65,581 (26.5)	21,858 (8.8)	10,735 (4.3)	247,247
2009	153,491 (60.9)	65,204 (25.8)	22,848 (9.1)	10,628 (4.2)	252,172
2010	186,881 (66.6)	60,207 (21.4)	24,693 (8.8)	8,848 (3.2)	280,636

Source: Citizenship and Immigration Canada (2009, 4–5), and Citizenship and Immigration Canada (2010). Figures for 2010 are preliminary.

residents who enter Canada solely or primarily for work and have obtained a work permit from [the department] to legally perform such activities" (2009, 47). As we have seen, such workers are used largely to fill gaps in the labour market and to facilitate growth and change in the economy. Foreign students, of course, are in Canada principally to study.

As Table 8 shows, the number of temporary foreign workers in Canada rose from just under 99,000 in 1984 to 363,000 by 2008, while the number of foreign students rose from 76,000 to almost 243,000, with both sources of temporary foreign residents increasing strongly in the mid- to later 1980s, again beginning in the later 1990s, and since 2004. Over the 2006–09 period, the top six source countries for temporary foreign workers were the United States (the largest source), Mexico, the Philippines, Australia, France, and the United Kingdom (Citizenship and Immigration Canada 2009, 59).

	Foreign Workers			Foreign Students		
	Entries	Still Present	Total	Entries	Still Present	Total
			(number)			
1984	65,175	33,573	98,748	26,832	48,870	75,702
1986	79,953	40,132	120,085	27,645	41,292	68,937
1988	99,308	51,661	150,969	36,515	40,786	77,301
1990	112,238	65,562	177,800	47,929	41,554	89,483
1992	108,870	63,503	172,373	52,954	45,894	98,848
1994	96,143	48,208	144,351	47,439	50,971	98,410
1996	89,760	53,818	143,578	46,587	65,136	111,723
1998	100,436	54,739	155,175	48,041	76,934	124,975
2000	116,565	61,458	178,023	69,104	89,906	159,010
2002	110,915	71,168	182,083	76,948	127,376	204,324
2004	112,553	86,450	199,003	66,121	150,161	216,282
2005	122,723	101,822	224,545	67,877	153,920	221,797
2006	139,103	116,886	255,989	71,786	156,246	228,032
2007	164,905	135,991	300,896	74,038	159,911	233,949
2008	192,519	170,975	363,494	79,509	163,352	242,861
2009	178,271	n.a.	n.a.	85,154	n.a.	n.a.
2010	182,322	n.a.	n.a.	96,147	n.a.	n.a.

Table 8: Temporary Foreign Workers and Foreign Students in Canada, 1984–2008

Source: Citizenship and Immigration Canada (2009, 48–49), and Citizenship and Immigration Canada (2011). Figures for 2010 are preliminary.

Immigrants in the Labour Market

What is the broad descriptive evidence of how well immigrants have done in the Canadian labour market after arrival? We start by looking at three measures of labour market involvement. The unemployment rate (UR) is the fraction of the population that is working or willing to work in the labour market but is currently jobless; it thus represents the degree of slack, and often hardship, in the labour market. The labour force participation rate (PR) is the fraction of the (age eligible) population that is working or willing to work in the labour market. A younger adult population, for example, typically has a high participation rate, while an elderly age group that includes many retirees has a very low participation rate. The employment rate (ER) is the fraction of the (age eligible) population that is employed in the labour market, and can be viewed as the utilization rate of available human resources within any group,

Table 9: Labour Market Involvement Rates of Immigrants Ages 25–54, by Sex, 2007

	Very Recent Immigrants	Recent Immigrants	Established Immigrants	Canadian -born
		(percent)		
Males				
Unemployment rate	10.1	6.6	5.2	5.0
Participation rate	86.4	91.3	92.2	91.4
Employment rate	77.7	85.2	87.4	86.8
Females				
Unemployment rate	12.3	8.1	5.5	4.1
Participation rate	61.3	74.4	81.8	84.3
Employment rate	53.8	68.4	77.3	80.8

Note: "Very recent" refers to immigrants who have been in Canada for five years or less, "recent" refers to immigrants who have been in Canada between five and ten years, "established" refers to immigrants who have been in Canada for more than ten years.
Source: Statistics Canada (2008, 10).

and hence the degree to which the group contributes to both the economy and household earnings.[1]

Results for these broad labour market involvement measures for immigrants are provided in Table 9 (by sex) and Table 10 (by education) for 2007. In both tables, immigrants are divided into "very recent" arrivals (those who have been in Canada for five years or less), "recent" arrivals (those who have been in Canada for between five and ten years), and "established" immigrants (those who have been in Canada for more than ten years), and compared with the Canadian-born.

Table 9 shows that unemployment rates among immigrants are higher than among Canadian-born workers, and their participation and employment rates are generally lower (except for established male immigrants). This reflects the difficulty that immigrants face in adjusting to, and getting economically established, in their new land and labour market environment. By these measures, female immigrants also experience greater adjustment difficulties and larger labour market involvement gaps relative to Canadian-born workers than do male immigrants. Also noticeable is that the gaps in labour market involvement between immigrants and Canadian-born workers of both sexes

---

1 A little bit of algebraic manipulation shows that these three measures are linked through the formula: ER = PR × [1 − UR]. The employment rate thus captures effects operating through both the participation rate and the unemployment rate.

Table 10: Labour Market Involvement Rates of Immigrants Ages 25–54 by Level of Education, 2007

	Very Recent Immigrants	Recent Immigrants	Established Immigrants	Canadian -born
		(percent)		
No degree, certificate,or diploma				
Unemployment rate	15.5	9.8	8.5	10.1
Participation rate	53.4	66.2	75.2	72.2
Employment rate	45.1	59.7	68.8	64.9
High school graduate				
Unemployment rate	12.6	6.5	6.2	4.8
Participation rate	71.5	74.0	83.8	86.2
Employment rate	62.3	69.2	78.6	82.1
Post-secondary certificate or diploma				
Unemployment rate	10.2	9.1	5.2	4.2
Participation rate	76.0	83.3	89.5	91.3
Employment rate	68.3	75.6	84.9	87.4
University degree				
Unemployment rate	10.7	6.2	3.6	2.4
Participation rate	75.3	87.5	91.3	92.9
Employment rate	67.3	82.1	88.0	90.7

Note: "Very recent" refers to immigrants who have been in Canada for five years or less, "recent" refers to immigrants who have been in Canada between five and ten years, "established" refers to immigrants who have been in Canada for more than ten years.
Source: Statistics Canada (2008, 20–23).

narrow significantly the longer immigrants remain in Canada. For example, the unemployment rate of very recent immigrants is more than twice that of Canadian-born males (three times as much for female immigrants), then declines from 10.1 to 6.6 percent for recent male immigrants, and then to 5.2 percent for established male immigrants — compared with an unemployment rate for the Canadian-born of 5.0 percent. That is, the labour market adjustment process that immigrants go through in becoming economically established in their new land is long term (more than ten years on average), but it is also front-loaded in that adjustment occurs fastest in the early years after landing and then continues at a slower rate the longer immigrants remain in Canada. The adjustment process also appears to be slower for female immigrants than for male immigrants.

Table 10 presents similar labour market involvement rates by level of education. In general, the higher the level of educational attainment, the greater the skill level of the workers and their attractiveness to employers, and hence the stronger the degree of labour market involvement. So, for Canadian-born workers, for example, the unemployment rate falls from 10.1 percent for those with less than high school completion to 2.4 percent for those with a university degree. Similarly, participation rates and employment rates rise with the level of education. Again, rates of labour market involvement of immigrants rise with length of time in Canada, with faster adjustment in the early years after arrival. But here we can also see that, among very recent immigrants, the weakness of their labour market involvement extends across all education levels. For very recent immigrants, the unemployment rate is 15.5 percent for those with less than high school graduation, and it is still 10.7 percent for university graduates. So, even those immigrants with considerable skills face an onerous adjustment process in becoming economically established. Thus, an immigration policy to attract higher-skilled workers will not show immediate economic effects. Over the long run, however, such a policy can be expected to result in the advancement of immigrants toward the labour market involvement levels of the Canadian-born population, though the process of adjustment is lengthy and, for many, incomplete.

Economic recessions also have major negative effects on immigrants' labour market involvement, earnings levels, and earnings growth rates, effects that are much more pronounced for male immigrants than for female immigrants. Abbott and Beach (2011) find that the early 1990s recession had marked and long-lasting effects on the earnings of immigrants arriving around that time. Picot (2010) estimates that, adjusting for age, education, and location of residence, the unemployment rate of Canadian-born men rose by 2.0 percentage points between August-October 2008 and August-October 2009, while that of recent immigrant men went up by 5.9 percentage points; over the same period, the employment rate of Canadian-born men fell by 2.1 points, while that of recent immigrant men went down by 9.8 points. Again, adjusting for age, education, and location of residence, Picot finds that recessionary unemployment rate increases over this same period were most severe among immigrants with lower levels of education. Canadian-born unemployment rates went up by 0.5 percentage points for those with a university degree and by 2.4 percentage points for those with a high school education or less. The corresponding unemployment rate increases among recent immigrants were 2.1 points and 14.8 points, respectively.

Figure 4 provides a display of immigrants' actual earnings (in constant 2004 dollars) upon entry and for years following their landing in Canada. The dashed lower line shows the average earnings of immigrant workers for

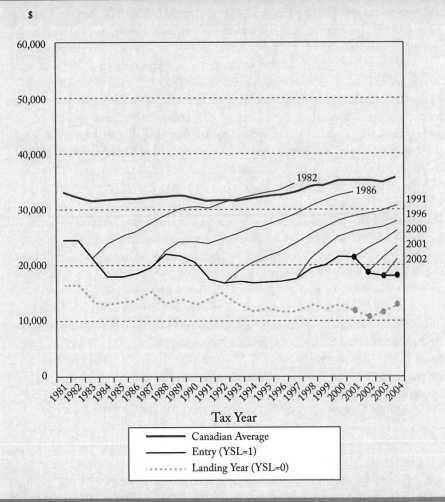

Figure 4: Average Annual Earnings of All Immigrants, by Year of Landing and Subsequent Working Years in Canada, 1981–2004

Tax Year

Legend:
- Canadian Average
- Entry (YSL=1)
- Landing Year (YSL=0)

Note: Dollar amounts are in 2004 dollars.
Source : Citizenship and Immigration Canada (2004, 3).

the calendar year in which they actually landed — that is, years since landing, or YSL = 0. It is low in part because it reflects only part-year earnings in Canada. The heavy line labelled "Entry" provides the average earnings of immigrant workers for their first full year after landing (YSL = 1). The lighter printed lines with dates attached to them show the average earnings growth of immigrant workers (YSL greater than 1) who arrived in Canada in the year attached to each such curve. So the line labelled 1982 indicates the

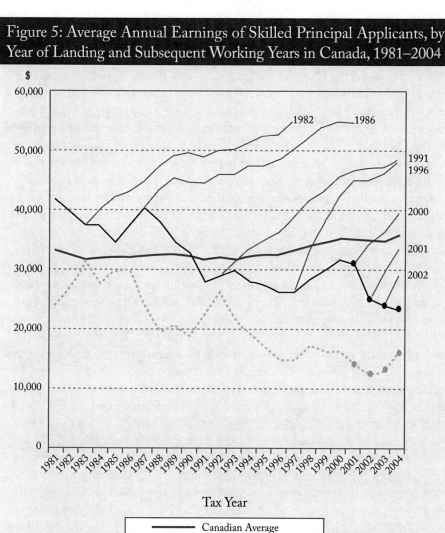

Figure 5: Average Annual Earnings of Skilled Principal Applicants, by Year of Landing and Subsequent Working Years in Canada, 1981–2004

Note: Dollar amounts are in 2004 dollars.
Source : Citizenship and Immigration Canada (2004, 7).

average earnings level each year from 1983 on for the 1982 landing cohort of immigrants. Its upward trend shows how the earnings of this cohort of immigrants adjusted toward the Canadian average earnings levels indicated in the upper solid line of the diagram.

Figure 4 shows some quite strong results on immigrant outcomes. The entry line shows that the effects of the early 1980s and early 1990s recessions and the early 2000s economic slowdown were much stronger on immigrant earnings than on the Canadian average line. But the entry line also has been generally declining since the early 1980s, in contrast to the average earnings of workers as a whole, which generally show a slight upward trend, at least since the early 1990s. Thus, the gap between immigrant entry earnings and the average earnings of Canadian workers as a whole has been widening markedly, largely as a result of which it is taking longer for immigrants' earnings to catch up to the Canadian average. For example, the 1982 cohort's average earnings caught up to the Canadian average by 1993 — that is, within 11 years of landing. But the lines for more recent landing cohorts are not narrowing the earnings gap nearly so rapidly. Indeed, the gap is now so large that recently arriving immigrants may no longer be able to catch up fully, and it remains for the second generation of immigrants to do so.

Further evidence on immigrant earnings adjustment is provided in Figure 5. The previous diagram was for all immigrant workers as a whole. But only a portion of all immigrants arrives in the Economic Class, and among that group the skills of only one member of the immigrant family are evaluated under the point system screen — that individual is referred to as the principal applicant. Figure 5 shows the earnings adjustment experience for such principal applicants. The explanation of the lines in the diagram is similar to Figure 4. Here, the earnings of principal applicants often exceed the Canadian average because the latter is averaged across all Canadian workers — both the comparably skilled and the less skilled. But the marked feature in Figure 5 is the significant decline in the average entry earnings levels of arriving principal applicants since the beginning of the 1980s, from well in excess of the Canadian average to well below, particularly since 2001; that is, from an average entry earnings level of about $42,000 in 1981 to about $24,000 by 2004 (in 2004 dollars). This decline is of considerable concern, and calls into question the success of the current system of selecting skilled immigrants.

Chapter 4

The Effects of Immigration Policy Levers on the Skills Characteristics of Canadian Immigrants

The development of an empirical framework for evaluating how well skilled immigrants are faring in the Canadian labour market in response to changes in major immigration policy levers involves three stages. The first stage is to examine how changes in policy levers affect the average skills levels of immigrants, the subject of this chapter.[1] The second stage is to analyze how immigrant workers' skills levels affect their average earnings levels in the Canadian labour market (Chapter 5). The framework of analysis thus allows one to distinguish between the effectiveness of immigration policy in attracting skilled workers and the experience of such immigrants in the Canadian labour market. The third stage then is to combine these two sets of results to estimate how changes in major policy levers ultimately affect average earnings levels of immigrants and the skills channels through which these effects operate (Chapter 6). Diagramatically, these three stages can be envisioned as:

Effects (policy lever on immigrant skills levels) ×
Effects (immigrant skills levels on immigrant earnings)
⟶   Effects (policy lever on immigrant earnings).

---

1   The presentation in this chapter summarizes the analysis and findings in Beach, Green, and Worswick (2008). The test results are presented in Appendix Tables A1–A3. The results for changing the Economic Class share of immigration are somewhat different from those in our earlier study because that paper used an indirect method of calculating that effect, whereas in this current study we use an improved direct method of calculation.

The first question to address is whether Canada's point system and key levers of immigration policy are effective in influencing the skills characteristics of arriving immigrants. Alternatively, how responsive are the skills characteristics of arriving immigrants to key policy levers? The key policy levers we examine in Beach, Green, and Worswick (2008) are, first, the total immigrant inflow in a given year; second, the share of this inflow arriving as Economic Class immigrants (that is, the proportion of immigrants arriving under the point system skills-evaluation screen); and, third, the weights within the point system allocated to three major skills dimensions: education level, age, and language fluency in English or French. These three policy levers are viewed as determining, or independent, variables that affect the skills outcomes of immigrants. The skills outcomes, or dependent, variables in the analysis are the education level of arriving immigrants, their age, and their language fluency in either (or both) of Canada's official languages. Here, age is viewed as an indicator of youth and, hence, a proxy for adaptability and flexibility to adjust to the Canadian labour market. The empirical analysis then involves estimating regression equations to test whether the three policy levers have identifiable effects on these three skills dimensions of arriving immigrants. The results can serve as a test of the effectiveness of the key immigration policy levers in Canada on the objective of raising average skills levels of arriving immigrants, and can offer lessons to other countries on the experience of Canadian immigration policy with a skills-based point system screen. As we outlined in Chapter 2, the 1980s and 1990s also saw major policy changes, and it would be useful to examine the effects those changes might have had on the skills characteristics of arriving immigrants.

Education, Age, and Language Fluency of Immigrants

As Table 11 shows, the education level of immigrants has risen significantly, with the proportion arriving with a university degree rising from 7.6 percent in 1980 to 34 percent by 2000, and that with only secondary education declining from 59 percent to just over 35 percent. Among Economic Class immigrants, the changes are more marked, as the proportion with a university degree rose from 12.3 percent to 47 percent over the period. For immigrants as a whole, the average years of education went up from about 9.7 years in 1980 to about 12.8 years by 2000. While education levels for the Canadian workforce as a whole also rose over this period, the increase was much faster for landing immigrants.

Figure 6 illustrates that there was a general reduction in immigrants' average age at landing between 1980 and 2004. Although the figure does not show it, the average age of Economic Class immigrants is about five years

Table 11: Level of Education of Immigrants on Landing, 1980, 1990, and 2000

Level of Education	Year of Landing		
	1980	1990	2000
	(proportion)		
All Immigrants			
University Post-graduate	.0177	.0289	.0902
University Undergraduate	.0583	.1100	.2506
Post-secondary	.1645	.1996	.1558
Secondary	.5898	.5316	.3526
Elementary or Less	.1676	.1297	.1507
Total landings (number)	143,136	216,402	227,313
Economic Class Immigrants			
University Post-graduate	.0333	.0438	.1337
University Undergraduate	.0900	.1365	.3364
Post-secondary	.2331	.2092	.1389
Secondary	.4900	.4797	.2258
Elementary or Less	.1508	.1308	.1652
Total landings (number)	49,895	95,627	133,422

Source: Authors' calculations from Beach, Green, and Worswick (2008).

younger than that for Family Class immigrants (26.3 years vs. 31.6 years). But the figure's most salient feature is the marked cyclical pattern where average age of arriving immigrants shoots up during recessions and then eases down over periods of economic expansion. Essentially, during expansions, Canada is an attractive destination for Economic Class immigrants, and since they are younger on average and often arrive as a family unit, this brings down the average age among all immigrants. During recessions, however, Canada becomes less attractive to Economic Class immigrants while the inflow of Family Class immigrants — who, on average, are older than those in the Economic Class and often involve parents — carries on apace.

Figure 7 illustrates that the pattern of change in rates of official language fluency of arriving immigrants over time is mixed, though perhaps showing a small increase, while Table 12 shows quite clearly that language fluency is

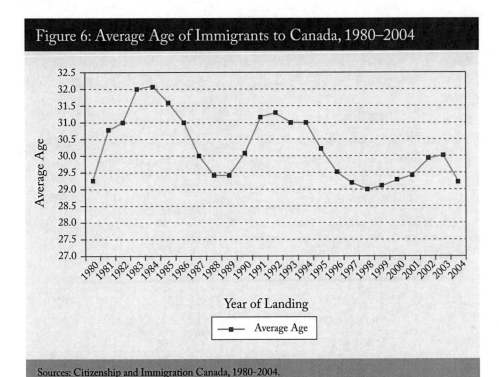

Figure 6: Average Age of Immigrants to Canada, 1980–2004

Year of Landing

Average Age

Sources: Citizenship and Immigration Canada, 1980-2004.

substantially greater among Economic Class immigrants than among others. The actual level of language fluency (in either English or French), however, is substantially lower among immigrants than among Canadian-born. Figure 8, which illustrates the estimated distributions of prose literacy scores for adult immigrants relative to Canadian-born males and females, shows that a much larger proportion of immigrants is at lower levels of literacy than is the case for Canadian-born workers, which as we will see, has important implications for immigration policy.

These descriptive results strongly suggest that increasing the share of the Economic Class of immigrants and hence the use of the point system, under which such immigrants are screened, raises the average skills level of immigrants. But it does so within the broader environment of immigration policy as a whole and of the general attractiveness of Canada to potential immigrants abroad.

Estimating the Effects of Policy Levers on Immigrants' Skills

Here, we formally test for the effects of key policy levers and point system

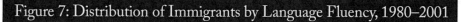

Figure 7: Distribution of Immigrants by Language Fluency, 1980–2001

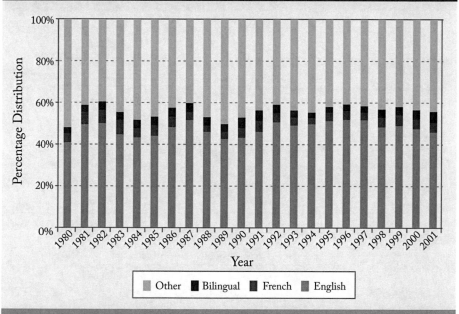

Source : Beach, Green and Worswick (2008).

Table 12: Language Fluency of Immigrants by Immigrant Class, 1980–2001

	English	French	Bilingual	Other
		(percent)		
Economic Class	54.1	4.7	5.5	35.7
Non-Economic Class	42.4	4.2	2.4	50.9
All immigrants	47.4	4.6	3.8	44.1

Source: Authors' calculations from Beach, Green, and Worswick (2008).

weights on the skills outcomes of immigrants, and estimate the magnitude of these effects. The specific questions we examine can be stated in terms of four hypotheses:

1. With respect to total immigration, does a larger immigration inflow rate reduce the overall skills level of an arriving cohort of immigrants as more arrive closer to the minimum pass mark requirement, or are likely to have a tougher time adjusting to the Canadian environment?

Figure 8: Distribution of Prose Literacy Scores for Immigrants and the Canadian-born

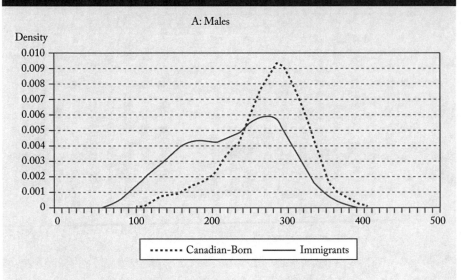

A: Males

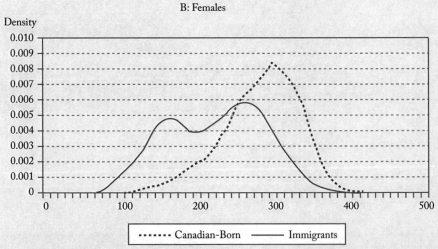

B: Females

Source: Bonikowska, Green, and Riddell (2008, 31, 33).

2. With respect to the composition of immigration, does an increase in the share of Economic Class immigrants raise the overall skills level of an arriving cohort of immigrants?

3. With respect to the point system, does an increase in the (maximum) point system weight on a particular skill dimension, such as level of education, have the desired effect of raising the overall skill level of arriving immigrants along this dimension?

4. With respect to business cycle effects, does a weaker labour market in Canada result in fewer skilled immigrants or a lower average skills level among arriving skilled immigrants, thus reducing the overall skills level, and does a weaker labour market in the United States, a substitute destination for immigrants, lead to an increase in the overall skills level of immigrants arriving in Canada?

To test these hypotheses, we estimate regression equations over individual arriving immigrants whose skills characteristics – education, age, fluency – are the dependent variables and with the above sets of policy levers as independent variables. The data set for this analysis is the Canadian Landings Data of all immigrants arriving in Canada for the years 1980 to 2001. This is not a sample; rather, it is the entire population of immigrant landings in Canada over that period.[2] Note also that the reported results all refer to the characteristics of immigrants at the time of landing, rather than at the time of application or processing.

The question immediately arises: to whom do these various hypotheses apply? Hypothesis 2, for example, is most relevant for the entire set of arriving immigrants. Hypotheses 3 and 4, however, are more relevant just to the set of Economic Class immigrants that enters under the point system screen. However, not all those classified as Economic Class immigrants are actually skills evaluated — only the family member designated as the "principal applicant." On average, 2.3 arrivals are classified as Economic Class immigrants for each arriving principal applicant.[3] So the cleanest test of the latter hypotheses actually would be just of the subset of principal applicant immigrants within the skilled worker and professionals category. We report results for both sets of immigrants — the former is the broadest with the largest number of observations and the latter is the smallest but offers the cleanest test of several of the above hypotheses.[4]

---

2 The Canadian Landings Data consists of just the landing information on each immigrant arriving over the 1980-2001 period. The all immigrants estimation sample for this study consists of all adult immigrants aged 20 or more at the time of their landing. The number of observations in this group is about 2.7 million immigrants over the entire period. The IMDB database, in contrast, is the merging of the individual Landings Data records with the immigrants' subsequent income tax records.

3 The number has risen slightly since the early 1980s, but has been relatively stable since the late 1980s. It also decreases slightly during recessions and rises again slightly in periods of economic expansion.

4 The number of all immigrant observations is about 2.8 million, and the number of observations in the principal applicants category is about 750,000 to 760,000, depending on which skill is being analyzed.

Appendix A presents three tables of regression results, one for each of the skills outcome dependent variables. Each table includes two regressions, one for all immigrants and one for the principal applicant sample. In addition to the results reported, the regressions also include controls for the source region of the immigrant (seven variables) and the region of residence in Canada of the immigrant upon landing (six variables).[5]

Turning first to the regression results on the education level of arriving immigrants, we see that increasing the total inflow of immigrants significantly reduces average education levels across both sample groups as more marginal applicants are attracted. Raising the total immigration level by 100,000 per year is estimated to reduce average years of education of all immigrants by 0.31 years, which supports hypothesis 1. Increasing the proportion of immigrants arriving under the Economic Class, rather than under family reunification or as refugees, raises average education levels for all immigrants: raising the share of the Economic Class by 10 percentage points increases average years of education for all immigrants by 0.26 years, thus supporting hypothesis 2. If we combine these two effects, we estimate that the effect of increasing the total level of immigrants by 100,000 solely by raising the number of those in the Economic Class — thus raising the current proportion of Economic Class immigrants from 60 percent to 71.4 percent — is virtually a wash, as the average education level for all immigrants falls by only 0.012 years, with the effect of the Economic Class share essentially counterbalancing the total-inflow effect.

Turning to the effect of the point system, increasing the (maximum) points allocated to education has a significantly positive effect on the sample of principal applicants, as one would expect. So, for example, raising education points by 10 percentage points (out of 100) within the point system is estimated to raise the average education level of principal applicants by at least 0.35 years, thus strongly supporting hypothesis 3. Giving points for having a university degree also raises education levels for the sample of principal

---

5 The all immigrants regressions also contain three controls for the admissions class under which the immigrant arrived. The education regressions also include a dummy variable for the years 1993 on, to capture the extra points awarded for a university degree (beyond simply years of education). The full set of regression results is available in Beach, Green, and Worswick (2008). More detailed explanations of the calculations of the estimated policy lever effects are provided in Appendix B.

A qualification of the results presented here is that changes in the total inflow of immigrants and in the share of the Economic Class are assumed to be exogenously determined by the authorities. If, however, the federal government were to base its policy changes on endogenous reactions to immigration outcomes, the reported results would be biased. More generally, the current approach to estimating policy effects is not based on classical controlled experiments or on quasi-experimental variations in the policy parameters.

applicants.[6] So, by combining these two effects, we estimate that the effect of a 10 percentage point increase in the weight of education plus points for having a university degree raises the average education level of principal applicants by 0.77 years. This is quite a strong effect, and it is not surprising that education levels and the proportion of immigrants with a university degree have been rising so rapidly.

The analysis also shows very robust business cycle effects on the education level of arriving immigrants. Since higher-skilled potential immigrants (applying under the Federal Skilled Worker Program, FSWP) are generally aware of relative employment and earnings opportunities among alternative destinations, a recession in Canada makes this country a less attractive destination for skilled immigrants and thus reduces the average education level of arriving immigrants. Conversely, a recession in the United States makes Canada relatively more attractive to skilled immigrants and raises the average level of education of immigrants arriving in Canada. Once again, these results strongly support hypothesis 4. Interestingly, the US unemployment rate effect is about twice as strong as the Canadian unemployment rate effect. A 3 percentage point rise in the Canadian unemployment rate — a marked recession — corresponds to a reduction in the average level of education of arriving principal applicants of 0.29 years, while a similar rise in the US unemployment rate increases principal applicants' level of education by 0.59 years. Thus, factors beyond Canadian policy that affect the relative attractiveness of Canada as a destination for immigrants can have quite major effects on the skills characteristics of immigrants actually landing here. A doubling of the US unemployment rate, as that country has experienced in the recent major recession, thus implies a considerable increase in the average education level of immigrants arriving in Canada.

The age of immigrants at time of landing is treated as a "skill" in that youth is taken as a proxy for flexibility and adaptability to the Canadian labour market. Since youth corresponds to lower age, the signs of the four hypotheses' effects are opposite to those found for the average education level. As Appendix Table A-2 shows, increasing the total inflow is estimated to raise the average age of immigrants in the principal applicant sample, though not for all immigrants. A 100,000 a year increase in the inflow rate raises the average age of principal applicants by 0.83 years. Raising the Economic Class share of immigrants reduces the average age of all immigrants, so a 10 percentage point increase in that share yields a 0.27 year reduction in the average age of all immigrants. Combining the two effects, we estimate that increasing the

---

6 See the 0.415 coefficient in the second column of Appendix Table A-1. We discuss this further in Chapter 6.

total level of immigration by 100,000 all within the Economic Class category reduces the average age of all immigrants by 0.60 years, as the two effects reinforce each other. As expected, an increase in age points within the point system also has a negative effect on the average age of principal applicants, so increasing that weight on age by, say, 10 percentage points yields a 0.17 year reduction in the average age of that category.

Business cycle effects are also substantial and highly statistically significant. A recession in Canada raises the average age of landing immigrants — see the pattern illustrated in Figure 6 — while a recession in the United States reduces average age of principal applicants. A 3 percentage point rise in the Canadian unemployment rate increases the average age of principal applicants by 1.54 years, while a similar rise in the US unemployment rate reduces the average age of principal applicants by 1.18 years. But here, the Canadian unemployment rate effect exceeds that of the US rate. Once again, though, the hypotheses are largely supported by their effects on the age of landing immigrants.

Since greater fluency in either English or French is a desirable skill, the expected signs of the effects of the four hypotheses should be the same as for the education skill dimension. The dependent variable is a 0-1 dummy for fluent versus non-fluent in either English or French. Given the large number of observations, we estimated these regressions as linear probability models, so the estimated dependent variable is interpreted as the proportion being fluent as a function of the independent variables. We estimate (see Appendix Table A-3) that increasing the total inflow of immigrants by 100,000 a year reduces the proportion of all immigrants fluent in either official language by 0.011, a statistically significant but rather weak effect. Raising the Economic Class share of immigrants, however, increases the proportion of all immigrants fluent in at least one official language — for example, a 10 percentage point increase in that share yields a 5.1 percentage point rise in the fluency rate of all immigrants, which is a quite strong effect. When we combine these two results, we estimate that a 100,000 increase in immigration levels completely within the Economic Class increases the official language fluency rate of arriving immigrants as a whole by 4.7 percentage points. In this case, the Economic Class share effect is much the dominant component. An increase in points allocated to language fluency within the point system again has a positive effect on actual fluency rates of principal applicants, so that increasing the weight on language fluency by 10 percentage points yields a 0.91 percentage point increase in the proportion of principal applicants who are fluent. So, the first three hypotheses again are supported in their effects on the degree of language fluency of arriving immigrants. A recession in Canada, however, is estimated to increase the degree of language fluency in both samples, while a recession in the United States again has the opposite effect. Why the pattern of business cycle effects in the case of language fluency is opposite to that of the other skill dimensions is not clear.[7] [8]

Conclusions and Implications

Several main conclusions follow from the above results. First, increasing the total inflow rate of immigrants lowers the average skills level of arriving cohorts of immigrants. Second, increasing the proportion of Economic Class immigrants (for a given rate of total inflow) raises the average skills level of all immigrants as a whole. Third, increasing the total level of annual immigration by raising just Economic Class admissions by that amount has virtually no effect on the average level of education of arriving immigrants, reduces their average age, and strongly increases their average rate of English- or French-language fluency. Fourth, business cycle effects on the skills level of immigrants are highly significant and generally operate so that a higher Canadian unemployment rate reduces the average skills level of arriving immigrants (with the exception of English-language fluency rates), and a higher US unemployment rate has the opposite effect (with the same exception). Fifth, increasing the weight on specific skills dimensions within the point system schedule indeed has the intended effect of raising the average skills level in each of these dimensions among arriving principal applicants in the skilled worker and professionals category. Basically, the point system works as intended.

---

7   Separate regressions run for French- and English-language fluency show that the expected pattern of hypothesis 4 indeed holds for French-language fluency, and the anomaly occurs only for English-language fluency. One possible explanation is that immigration officers, who have some discretion in awarding points for language fluency, may demand higher standards in awarding points for English fluency during a recession but ease up during an economic expansion. When there is a recession in the United States, a greater number of highly skilled applicants applies to enter Canada, and immigration officers may be happy to accommodate them even to the point of lowering language standards. Applicants who are fluent in French are likely less common and treated in a more conventional fashion similar to education. (We owe the suggestion of this interpretation to Professor Weili Ding at Queen's University.) Another possible explanation is a selection effect by possible applicants: people with very limited English or French proficiency may choose not to come to Canada during a recession, while those with language fluency may be undeterred.

8   Unfortunately, the linear specifications reported in Appendix Tables A-1 through A-3 do not allow us to estimate whether there is a level of immigration that, say, maximizes earnings of arriving immigrants, or to identify a threshold level of immigration beyond which such earnings fall off markedly. One approach to addressing this issue might be to estimate a more general set of regression results that would include a quadratic term in LOM. However, we would want to give some thought as to how such levels might change through time, and an optimal or threshold level for one skill dimension might be quite different for another dimension. We leave this as an agenda for possible further research.

It is important to note at this juncture that the term "Economic Class" used in the results of this section effectively refers to the FSWP, and that the landings data underlying this study come from the period 1980–2001. At that time, the Provincial Nominee Program was minor (accounting for less than 1 percent of all Economic Class immigrants in 2001, for example) and the Canadian Experience Class initiative did not exist. So, in 2001, the FSWP accounted for more than 88 percent of all Economic Class immigrants (Citizenship and Immigration Canada 2010). Consequently, in the above conclusions, one can read "Economic Class" immigrants to mean immigrants landing under the FSWP.

What can we say about the relative effectiveness of our alternative policy levers? In fact, there is no single way to measure the relative effectiveness of different policy levers, skills outcomes, and sample groups, so we consider two alternative approaches.

In the first approach, we look at the relative strength of policy levers on skills outcomes as measured by the percentage change in skills outcomes for a given specified change in the policy lever.[9] In the case of the total inflow of immigration, we consider the effect of increasing it by 100,000 a year (keeping constant the immigrant class mix) — see the first row of Table 13. In the case of the Economic Class share, we consider the effect of increasing the proportion of those immigrants, who arrive under the point system, by 10 percentage points (holding constant the total inflow rate) — see the second row of Table 13. Next, we look at the combined effect of increasing the total inflow of immigrants by 100,000 per year with the increase occurring solely in the Economic Class — see the third row of Table 13. Finally, in the case of changing skills weights awarded within the point system, we consider — in the bottom row of Table 13 — the effect of increasing the maximum points for a given skill dimension by 10 percentage points (relative to the required pass mark). In the latter case, we look at the effects on the skill outcomes of the principal applicants themselves. So, for example, we estimate that a 100,000 increase in the total inflow of immigration reduces the average level of education among all immigrants by 2.8 percent. A larger number means a stronger relative effect within a given row for a given policy lever change. The effects of different policy lever changes on a given skill outcome are shown in the columns of Table 13. So, for example, the assumed increase in immigration inflow is estimated to change the language fluency rate of arriving immigrants by 2.0 percent, while the assumed increase in point system weights for language proficiency is found to change the fluency rate by 1.2 percent.

---

9 In calculating the percentage changes in skills outcome measures, we used the following averages: for all immigrants, Avg ED = 11, Avg AGE = 29, and Avg LF = 0.56; for principal applicants, Avg ED = 13, Avg AGE = 26, and Avg LF = 0.75.

Table 13: Relative Strength of Policy Levers in Changing Immigrants' Skills Outcomes

Policy Lever	Skill Characteristic		
	Education	Age at Landing	Language Fluency
	(absolute value of % change in skill outcome)		
Total inflow[a]			
All immigrants	2.8	1.0	2.0
Economic Class share[b]			
All immigrants	2.4	0.9	9.0
Combined effect[c]			
All Immigrants	0.1	2.1	8.3
Point system weights[d]			
Principal Applicants	2.7	0.7	1.2

a "Total inflow" refers to raising the total inflow of immigrants by 100,000 per year.
b "Economic Class share" refers to increasing the proportion of immigrants arriving in the Economic Class category by 10 percentage points.
c "Combined Effect" refers to the effect of increasing the total inflow of immigrants by 100,000 per year solely by raising the numbers in the Economic Class.
d "Point system weights" refers to the effect of increasing the maximum points (within the point system) for a given skill dimension by 10 percentage points relative to the pass mark on that respective skill.
Source: Authors' calculations based on estimated coefficients in Tables A-1, A-2, and A-3.

A second approach to illustrating the relative strength of policy levers on skills outcomes is to ask how large a policy lever change would be required to generate a given specified change in average outcomes. In the case of education, the issue is how large a change in each policy lever would be needed to raise the average level of education by six months. The answers are shown in the first column of Table 14. In the case of the age outcome, the required change is to lower the average age of arriving immigrants by six months. The policy lever changes needed to generate this result are shown in the second column of the table. And the figures in the third column indicate the size of the policy lever changes required to increase the average level of language fluency (in either English or French) of arriving immigrants by 0.5 of a percentage point. Obviously in Table 14, smaller numbers indicate greater relative strength. So, for example, it takes either an increase in total immigration levels by 161,000 a year or a 14.1 percentage point increase in the education weight in the point system schedule to change the average level of education of incoming immigrants by six months.

Table 14: Relative Strength of Policy Levers in Achieving Specific Changes to Immigrants' Skills Outcomes

Policy Lever	Skill Characteristic		
	Education	Age at Landing	Language Fluency
	(change required to generate given change in skill outcome)		
Total inflow[a]			
All immigrants	161,000	172,000	45,500
Economic Class share[b]			
All immigrants	19.3 pts	18.3 pts	0.99 pts
Point system weights[c]			
Principal Applicants	14.1 pts	29.3 pts	5.49 pts

a "Total inflow" refers to the increase in thousands of immigrant landings per year required to generate a change in the average education level of all immigrants by half a year, or a change in the average age of all immigrants by half a year, or a change in the average fluency rate (in either English or French) by 0.5 of a percentage.
b "Economic Class share" refers to the increase in the share of Economic Class immigrants (out of the total inflow) required to generate a change in the average education level of all immigrants by half a year, or a change in the average age of all immigrants by half a year, or a change in the average fluency rate (in either English or French) by 0.5 of a percentage point.
c "Point system weights" refers to the increase in the maximum points given within the point system (relative to the pass mark) to a particular skill required to generate a change in the average education level of principal applicants by half a year, or a change in the average age of principal applicants by half a year, or a change in the average fluency rate (in either English or French) among principal applicants by 0.5 of a percentage point.
Source: Authors' calculations based on estimated coefficients in Tables A-1, A-2, and A-3.

While these two approaches to measuring the relative strength of different policy levers yield generally similar results, they are not identical because they are based on different questions. Nonetheless, several general conclusions follow. First, no single policy lever dominates across all skills measures. Total inflow and point system weights have a significant effect on immigrants' average education level, for example, while increasing the Economic Class share has a very strong effect on the average language fluency of arriving immigrants. Second, policy lever effects on the education level and language fluency are relatively strong, but their effects on age are relatively weak. This might reflect that maximum age points are allocated for a fairly broad age interval, then decrease symmetrically for young and old — that is, those on both sides of the maximum-age-point interval — whereas for education and language fluency more is preferred to less — that is, the decrease occurs on only one side of the maximum-point levels. Third, across all three sets of policy levers, language fluency is most responsive to changes in general, the education level is somewhat less responsive, and the age of landing immigrants is significantly the least responsive. More specifically, the effect on language fluency of increasing the Economic Class share is about the strongest estimated effect, while that of increasing the point system weight for age is about the weakest. Finally, the combined effects sometimes counter each other, as in the case of education and language fluency, and sometimes reinforce each other, as in the case of age.

Note also that increasing the point system weight for one skill also might have cross effects on other skills. Our earlier study (Beach, Green, and Worswick 2008), for example, reveals that, since highly educated immigrants are more likely to be proficient in English or French, raising the point system weight on years of education or having a university degree also increases the rate of official language fluency. Or, since more education takes longer to obtain, an increased weight on education also results in older immigrants on arrival.[10]

It also might be useful to compare the relative strengths of our policy lever effects to some effects of the policy environment itself. Specifically, we look at the relative strengths of Canadian and US business cycle effects as represented by the two countries' respective unemployment rates. The upper panel of Table 15 shows the effects of a 3 percentage point increase in either the Canadian or US unemployment rate, expressed in terms of percentage changes in the average skills outcome variables of principle applicant immigrants. One can see immediately that these unemployment rate effects are really quite substantial, both in their own right and compared with the policy lever effect. And the sensitivity of the average rate of language fluency to both Canadian and US unemployment rates is markedly the strongest. Indeed, a 3 percentage point change in unemployment rates is not unheard of — in the recent major recession, the Canadian unemployment rate rose by 2.7 percentage points (from January 2008 to August 2009) while the US rate went up by a substantial 5.6 points (from 2007 to the third quarter of 2009).[11] The effects of combining these two changes in unemployment rates are presented in the lower two rows of Table 15 in percentage changes (penultimate row) and actual amounts (last row), and are remarkably strong, particularly since they are estimated to occur over a period of recession. The average education level of incoming principal applicants is estimated to rise and the average age to decline, but the average rate of language fluency declines as well. So the

---

10 The simpler results in Appendix Tables A1–A3, however, do not incorporate these various cross effects.

11 Canadian Economic Observer (February 2010, 18 and 71.)

Table 15: Relative Strength of Canadian and US Unemployment Rates in Changing Immigrants' Skills Outcomes

	Education	Age at Landing	Language Fluency
	(absolute value of % change in skills outcomes of principal applicants of a 3 percentage point increase in the unemployment rate)		
Canadian unemployment rate	2.2	5.9	17.1
US unemployment rate	4.5	4.5	17.3
	(% change in skills outcomes of principal applicants of change in Canadian and US unemployment rates between pre- and peak-recession levels)		
Combined effect	+6.4	−3.1	−16.8
	(change in levels of skills outcomes of principal applicants of change in Canadian and US unemployment rates between pre- and peak-recession levels)		
Combined effect	+0.84 (years)	−0.81 (years)	−.13 (proportion)

Source: Authors' calculations based on estimated coefficients in Tables A-1, A-2, and A-3.

principal conclusion to be drawn here is that changes in the environment of Canada's immigration application process can have quite major effects on the skills outcomes of immigrants.

In the next chapter, we examine the effects of immigrants' skills characteristics at the time of landing on their subsequent post-arrival earnings outcomes. Combined with the results in this chapter on the effects of policy lever changes on immigrants' skills outcomes, this allows us in Chapter 6 to draw conclusions about the effects of different policy levers in determining immigrants' earnings after their arrival in Canada.

The Effects of Immigrants' Skills Characteristics on Their Earnings

Chapter 5

Immigrants' success in the Canadian labour market depends on the skills they bring with them when they land in Canada as well as on personal characteristics, the transferability of their human capital and credentials, their work habits, the economic and social environment of their new country and area of residence, and simple chance. Thus, if we want to understand more fully the long-run effects of immigration policy levers on immigrants' success, we also need to look at how immigrants fare after their arrival. The literature on immigrant adjustment and outcomes in Canada and elsewhere is enormous and overlaps many disciplines; we therefore narrow our focus to the more conventional economic outcome of immigrants' labour market earnings.

How have immigrants done in terms of their labour market earnings as a function of their skills characteristics at the time of landing? We know — as it has been a subject of major inquiry in the research literature — that the earnings of immigrants relative to those of non-immigrants have been slipping over the past few decades, despite the rise in immigrant skills levels. So an analysis of the relationship between landing characteristics and post-landing earnings outcomes cannot be handled by looking at a simple cross-sectional census-type window of outcomes for a given year. Instead, we take account of the time of arrival of immigrants by again making use of published estimates based on a major Canadian database — in this case, the so-called IMDB database, which follows the earnings of immigrants after their arrival in Canada for research purposes. This database combines landing characteristics of immigrants, including their date of arrival, with their subsequent earnings outcomes through time.[1]

---

1 The material in this chapter follows from Green and Worswick (2002).

Estimates of Immigrants' Earnings in Canada

The basis for analyzing the effects of workers' skills on the earnings they are paid is the standard human capital model. Developed by Becker (1964) and Mincer (1974), among others, the basic idea is that workers are paid more the more productive they are in the labour market, and two key dimensions of this productivity are a worker's education and cumulated work experience. Both education and work experience, or on-the-job training, as it is often called, are acquired through an investment process that involves forgone earnings for the time spent learning and explicit educational and training costs such as tuition and training manuals. The terms "skilled workers" and "highly skilled workers" in the literature and in this volume, thus refer to workers who have acquired extensive learning and training at school and on the job. These human capital characteristics can be viewed as important inputs into the production of valuable cognitive and non-cognitive skills that make workers productive in the labour market, rather than as objective measures of such skills per se (Ferrer, Green and Riddell 2006).

Human capital investment in skill acquisition provides the greatest return if it is made early in a career, when there is the longest possible payback period and when the opportunity cost of a worker's time is relatively low (in terms of what the worker could otherwise have earned in the labour market), compared with the value of the worker's time in, say, mid-career. Formal education typically is incurred before entering the labour market full time. On-the-job training generally is spread over a number of years — with the amount differing according to the type of occupation and career path a worker follows — but again the typical pattern is to learn a lot early in the work career to maximize the pay-back period and reduce the opportunity cost of the worker's time in the labour market. This approach can be expressed as a so-called earnings or wage equation where the left-hand side shows a worker's earnings or wages as dependent, or outcome, variables, and on the right-hand side, the level of education (ED) and cumulated amount of work experience (EXP) appear — along with other possible determining factors — as independent, or explanatory, variables. To capture the idea that the rate of investment in on-the-job training is likely to decrease with length of work experience, the work experience variable typically appears quadratically — that is, EXP and EXP^2. ED and EXP are expected to appear in an earnings equation with positive coefficients and EXP^2 with a negative coefficient, indicating that ED and EXP have positive direct effects on a worker's earnings, and that the EXP effect of an additional year of work experience becomes smaller as more experience has already been accumulated.

The standard human capital model has been extended — by Chiswick (1978) and Borjas (1985, 1995b), among others — to incorporate the earnings adjustment process of immigrants after landing in their new country.[2] Chiswick argues that, initially after arrival, immigrants lack the familiarity with North American labour markets of native-born workers, have a very limited (if any) network of possible employers and employment options, and may have only limited fluency in the language of the receiving country, so that their earnings levels shortly after arrival are typically substantially below those of their native-born peers who have similar levels of education and work experience. However, like young workers entering the full-time labour market, they invest in new skills that are especially useful in their adopted labour market, such as becoming more fluent in the local tongue and developing a more extensive network of employment connections and work options, and work hard to get ahead in their new land.

Applying Chiswick's theory to the Canadian case, we find that immigrants' earnings in the labour market increase at a faster rate than those of their Canadian-born peers, thus narrowing the earnings gap between the two groups with the same years of education and total work experience the longer immigrants stay in Canada. Eventually, since immigrants are likely self-selected to be more able and motivated, their average earnings might even overtake those of the Canadian born if they continue to work hard to get ahead and if some of the less successful among them return home or move on to another country.

One can capture these basic arguments within a human capital earnings equation framework by adding additional explanatory variables in the form of a dummy variable for whether or not a worker is an immigrant ("immigrant status dummy") and a variable for the number of years since an immigrant's landing (or YSL). Since the YSL variable operates in exactly the same way as the standard EXP variable, one would also include the YSL variable quadratically. The expectation is that the coefficient on the immigrant status dummy would be negative since the initial earnings of immigrants post arrival are less than those of their Canadian-born peers. The coefficients on YSL and YSL^2 would be positive and negative, respectively, as work experience in their new home increases immigrants' earnings at a faster pace than that of their Canadian-born peers, though the rate of this faster pace declines as immigrants assimilate into the Canadian labour market. This pattern of the earnings gap between immigrants and Canadian-born workers is illustrated in Figure 9.

Borjas (1985), however, points out that different cohorts of immigrants have different experiences depending on when they arrived in their new land,

---

2 An overview can be found in Benjamin et al. (2007).

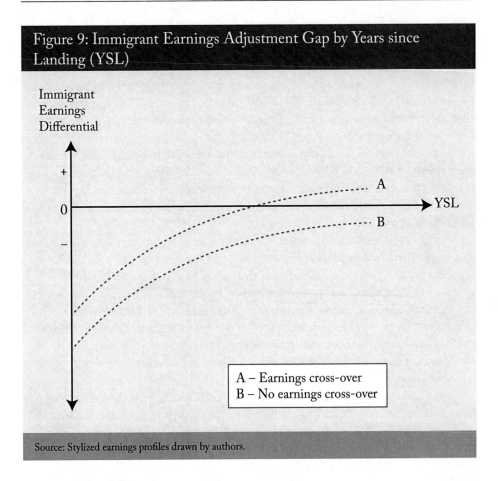

Figure 9: Immigrant Earnings Adjustment Gap by Years since Landing (YSL)

Immigrant Earnings Differential

A – Earnings cross-over
B – No earnings cross-over

Source: Stylized earnings profiles drawn by authors.

and that an appropriate way to capture these different post-arrival earnings-adjustment experiences is to use longitudinal data that follows individual workers through time. This is the approach from which the study by Green and Worswick (2002) begins.

Green and Worswick make use of the IMDB database that links Canadian immigrant landing records and income tax records essentially for the tax years 1981–97. For Canadian-born workers, they use data from the Canadian Surveys of Consumer Finances (SCF) for the same years. They organize their data for both immigrants and Canadian-born according to labour market entry cohort. They define five entry cohorts: 1980–82, 1983–86, 1987–89, 1990–92, and 1993–96. Immigrants are assigned to a cohort according to the year they landed in Canada. Canadian-born workers are assigned to a cohort based on the year in which they turned 25, as a means of capturing their entry into the mature labour market in Canada. The authors combine the two microdata sets by a synthetic cohort analysis of 2,442 data cells broken down by entry cohort, education level, income year, and, for immigrants, age at time of landing and admission class. To avoid further issues of joint household labour supply — such as related work patterns between husband and wife — Green and Worswick report only for men in the labour market between the ages of 25 and 64.

Regression results for immigrant and Canadian-born men are presented in Appendix Table A-4. The dependent variable is expressed in terms of log earnings, so that the regression coefficients can be interpreted essentially as proportional or percentage effects. For example, workers with only high school education are estimated to earn 23 percent less, on average, than those with post-secondary training, and university graduates are estimated to earn 26 percent more, on average, than those with post-secondary training. Work experience over a career also shows the expected general upward-sloping concave pattern (with a positive coefficient on EXP and a negative coefficient on EXP^2) for which the standard human capital model argues.

The portion of Appendix Table A-4 of most interest, however, is the first three sets of coefficients. The first column reports results for a simpler specification. The shape of the immigrant earnings adjustment profile illustrated in Figure 10 is given by the immigrant status dummy variable coefficient and the two years-since-landing coefficients, which show an upward sloping but concave earnings gap profile. The negative cohort coefficients in the first column — the intercept of the YSL earnings adjustment curve in Figure 10 — show that the YSL profile for more recently arriving cohorts of immigrants has been shifting down, so that the earnings gap between immigrant and Canadian-born workers indeed widened over the 1980s and 1990s.

The results in the second column are for a more general specification. In this case, the slope of the YSL earnings adjustment profile curve (as well as the intercept) has shifted across the different arrival cohorts. While the curve indeed has shifted down significantly over the period, its slope — as indicated by the cohort-YSL interaction coefficients — has been rising. That is, as illustrated in Figure 10, the immigrant adjustment earnings profile curve has shifted: the earnings gap has widened as more recent cohorts of immigrants slip further behind their Canadian-born peers, and although the rate of year-to-year immigrant earnings increase has risen, it has not been enough to counter the general downward shift of the curve.

Let us now investigate how the earnings adjustment profile of immigrants was affected by their education, age, and language fluency at their time of landing in Canada. Appendix Table A-5 presents separate earnings adjustment regressions broken down by three education levels and four age-at-landing groups. We follow the more general specification from the second column

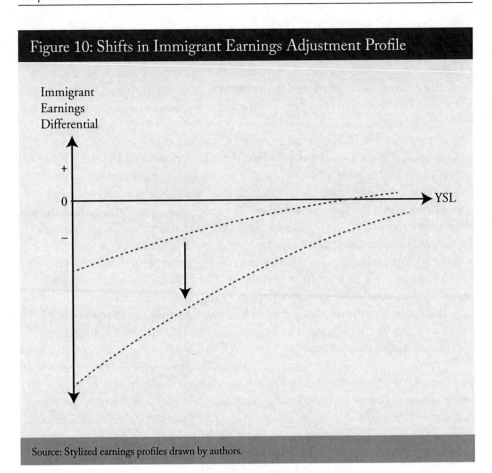

Figure 10: Shifts in Immigrant Earnings Adjustment Profile

Immigrant
Earnings
Differential

+

0   YSL

–

Source: Stylized earnings profiles drawn by authors.

of Table A-4 in allowing for cohort-YSL interactions — that is, both the intercept and the slope shift in the earnings adjustment curve.[3]

We turn first to education. Several observations from the results in Table A-5 stand out. First, for the 1980–82 arrival cohort, the earnings of immigrants with a university education initially were higher than those of Canadian-born workers, while the earnings of immigrants with only a high school education initially were lower than those of their Canadian-born peers. So the earnings gap was most detrimental for immigrants with lower levels of education — that is, the education differential in earnings was larger among immigrants than non-immigrants. For the most recent 1993–96

---

3 One can calculate, from the results in column 2 of Table A-4, that the number of years required for immigrants' earnings on average to catch up to those of Canadian-born workers has risen from 21 years for the 1980–82 arrival cohort to about 90 years for the 1993–96 arrival cohort — in effect, the latter cohort will not catch up in its own generation.

cohort, the earnings gap[4] was still largest (in percentage terms) for those with less education, and the education differential in earnings was still wider for immigrant workers than for Canadian-born workers. Second, the initial earnings gap for immigrants worsened much more dramatically across cohorts for university graduates than for immigrants with a high school education.[5] Alternatively, the immigrant earnings adjustment profile shifted down much faster for those with the highest levels of education — that is, more educated immigrants were having a harder time getting ahead than did earlier cohorts of such immigrants. As well, the education differential in earnings has narrowed more among immigrants than among non-immigrants. This is, of course, consistent with a marked ongoing increase in the supply of university-educated workers to the Canadian workforce as well as an increasing supply of university-educated immigrants. Third, the slopes of the immigrant adjustment profiles are generally not statistically significant among university-educated immigrants, nor have they changed significantly across arriving cohorts of high-school- and university-educated immigrants. So the observed widening of initial earnings gaps among immigrants was not made up by steeper or faster earnings adjustment gains. Only by the 1993–96 cohort did the slope of the university-educated immigrant adjustment profile turn significantly positive.

Turning next to immigrants' age at arrival, we again present three corresponding results in Appendix Table A-5. First, for the 1980–82 arrival cohort, the initial size of the earnings gap worked in favour of older arriving immigrants (who had more former work experience) and was more detrimental for younger arriving immigrants (who had less experience). That is, the work-experience differential in earnings at time of arrival was also larger among immigrants than among Canadian-born workers. By the 1993–96 arrival cohort, however, the initial earnings gap no longer favoured one skill group or the other as the percentage immigrant earnings differential was more or less similar across all four age-at-arrival groups[6] for a given education level. Second, the initial earnings gap worsened much more dramatically across cohorts among older, more experienced arrivals than for younger, less experienced arrivals.[7] So the immigrant earnings adjustment profile shifted down much faster for those with greater amounts of work

---

4 Calculated by adding the coefficient for "1993–96 cohort" to that for the "Immigrant Status" dummy.

5 Indicated by the larger negative coefficients on the cohort dummies for university graduates than for high-school-educated immigrants.

6 Indicated by the larger negative coefficients on the cohort dummies for older arriving immigrants than for younger arriving immigrants.

7 Calculated by adding the coefficient for the 1993-96 cohort to that for the immigrant status dummy.

experience — that is, older, more experienced immigrants at time of arrival had a harder time getting ahead than earlier cohorts of immigrants. The work experience differential in earnings narrowed more among immigrants than among Canadian-born workers, or there was a narrowing of the age-earnings differential among immigrants at the time of landing. This, in turn, is consistent with the large, ageing baby boom cohort of workers. Indeed, the worsening immigrant earnings differential by higher levels of education and work experience interacted to yield the very large negative cohort coefficients for older, university-educated immigrants shown in Table A-5. This is consistent with media stories of middle-aged, foreign-trained immigrant university graduates unable to find well-paying jobs in Canada commensurate with their skills and training. Third, the slopes of the immigrant earnings profiles decline — or even become more negative — for older arriving immigrants. This is generally what would be expected from a human capital perspective, as older workers have less incentive to invest time and effort to build up their host-country skills than do younger immigrants because they have a shorter expected pay-back horizon. Most of the cohort changes in slope coefficients, however, are not statistically significant.

The results in Table A-5 are for immigrants as a whole. Skills-related effects, though, are more likely to show up among Economic Class immigrants, and even more so among principal applicants within that class. Accordingly, the results are recalculated just for principal applicant immigrants (as compared to Canadian-born workers); see Appendix Table A-6.[8] Essentially, the first two results above for both education and age-at-arrival of immigrants hold even more markedly. The immigrant earnings gap was most detrimental at lower levels of education and for younger arriving immigrants (those with lower skills levels), so that skills differentials in earnings were larger among arriving immigrants than among Canadian-born workers. Also, the initial immigrant earnings gap worsened across cohorts most markedly for university graduates and for older, more experienced immigrants (those at higher skills levels) at the time of arrival, so that skills differentials in earnings narrowed more among immigrants than among Canadian-born workers over the period.

Becoming fluent in an official language is a form of human capital investment that provides economic benefits over a working career; further, a large literature shows that, in the Canadian context, becoming bilingual pays dividends in terms of higher earnings.[9] The same argument holds even more

---

8 Since most of the slope-cohort-interaction coefficients were not statistically significant before, these slope interaction terms were excluded from the regressions in Table A-6.

9 See, for example, Vaillancourt (1980); Christofides and Swidinsky (2010); and Nadeau (2010).

for immigrants.[10] The converse, then, is that weaker proficiency in a official language is associated with lower earnings than otherwise, perhaps because of fewer and less remunerative job options, or the inability to handle as many tasks as quickly or correctly, or even the presence of discrimination or lack of understanding of foreign qualifications in the labour market. Direct estimates in the research literature support the assertion that weaker proficiency in either English or French in Canada is indeed associated with substantially lower earnings by immigrants. For example, Ferrer, Green, and Riddell (2006) find that the average difference in document literacy scores between Canadian-born and immigrant workers with only foreign education is associated with lower male immigrant earnings by 21.6 percent.[11]

A proxy for language fluency could be taken from the country of origin of arriving immigrants. Figures 11, 12, and 13 present cohort shifts in the YSL-earnings adjustment curve between three groupings of countries of origin.[12] Figure 11 refers to the English-speaking countries of the United States, United Kingdom, Australia, and New Zealand; Figure 12 refers to the northwestern European countries of France, Germany, Holland, Denmark, Belgium, Switzerland, Sweden, and Norway; and Figure 13 refers to all other countries of origin. As we saw in Figure 1 (Chapter 3), since 1980 there has been a major decline in the proportion of immigrants coming from the first two groups of countries and a corresponding increase in the share coming from the third group.

It is immediately apparent that the negative initial earnings gap between arriving immigrants and Canadian-born workers is largely restricted to arrivals from the third group of countries (Grady 2010 obtains a similar result). That is, once again, the immigrant earnings differential is wider or more detrimental for those with "more foreign" skills. Admittedly, language might not be the only reason for such differentials, as such immigrants could have skills and backgrounds that simply are harder to match to the demands of the Canadian labour market. Nonetheless, the shifting composition of immigrants toward the third group of countries of origin is likely a major contributor to the generally widening average immigrant earnings differential illustrated in Figure 10. Within each group of countries, however, there is evidence of a worsening initial immigrant earnings gap, occurring most markedly over the

---

10 See, for example, Dustmann and Fabbri (1995); and Chiswick and Miller (2007, 2008).

11 The authors obtain this figure by multiplying the average document literacy score differential for the two groups (288 − 216 = 72) in their Table 1 by the literacy score effects on earnings (0.003) in column 4 of their Table 3. Bonikowska, Green, and Riddell (2008, 2010) obtain a generally similar result.

12 The histograms in Figures 11, 12, and 13 show the sets of arrival cohort intercept coefficients from regressions such as in Appendix Table A-5.

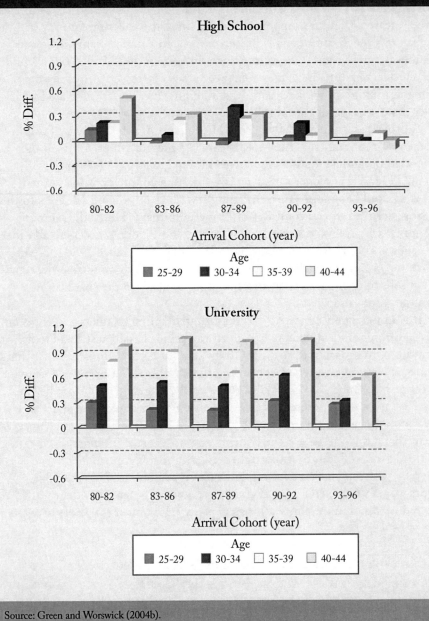

Figure 11: Earnings Differences between the Canadian-born and Immigrants from English-Language Countries in Their First Year after Arrival, by Age and Education Level, 1980–96

High School

% Diff.

Arrival Cohort (year)

Age
25-29   30-34   35-39   40-44

University

% Diff.

Arrival Cohort (year)

Age
25-29   30-34   35-39   40-44

Source: Green and Worswick (2004b).

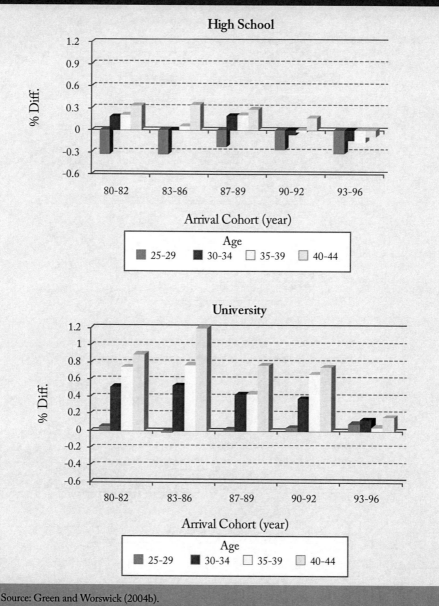

Figure 12: Earnings Differences between the Canadian-born and Immigrants from Non-English-speaking Northwest European Countries in Their First Year after Arrival, by Age and Education Level, 1980–96

Source: Green and Worswick (2004b).

Figure 13: Earnings Differences between the Canadian-born and Immigrants from Non-English-speaking Countries Outside Northwest Europe in Their First Year after Arrival, by Age and Education Level, 1980–96

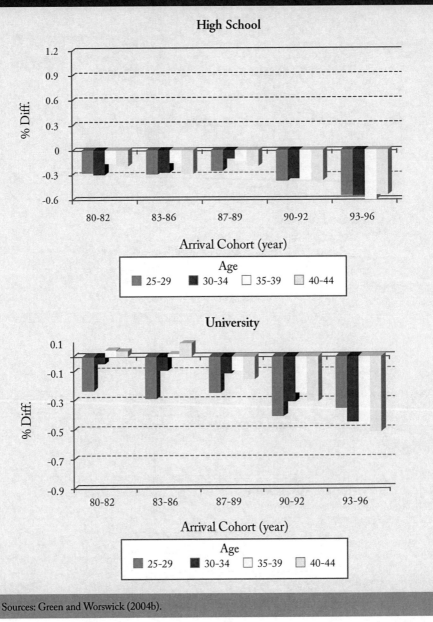

Sources: Green and Worswick (2004b).

1990s. So the shifting composition of immigration toward the "more foreign" group of countries cannot be the whole story. Also, while the worsening of the immigrant earnings differential by education and work experience is most marked among the higher skilled, in the cases of language fluency and the "more foreignness" of immigrants' origin, the worsening evidently has occurred right across the spectrum of workers.

Changing Returns to Immigrants' Skills

Since the early 1980s, as has been well documented,[13] the earnings of immigrants at their time of arrival have been declining relative to the earnings of Canadian-born workers. The declines are also related to key dimensions of labour market skills such as education, work experience, and language fluency at the time immigrants arrive in Canada. A good deal of debate has revolved around what economists call the "returns", or higher earnings, to foreign education and work experience immigrants acquire before arriving in Canada and their degree of English or French language fluency upon landing.

By "returns" to skills or to human capital, economists mean the average increase in the earnings of workers — usually in percentage terms — from having a greater degree or higher level of some labour market skill such as years of education, years of work experience in the labour market, or degree of fluency in the host country's official language(s). Such returns are typically measured by statistical regression analysis, which holds constant other factors that also could affect earnings levels, such as gender, age, race, location of residence (whether urban or rural), length of time since immigration to Canada, and possibly occupation and full-time/part-time work status. Earnings differentials by various skills measures can be estimated in terms of the entry earnings of immigrants shortly after their arrival in Canada.

The returns to skills depend on many factors:

- the skills' productivity or usefulness in the Canadian labour market;
- the demand for and supply of such skills available in Canada;
- the level of skills the immigrant possesses and the work the immigrant ends up obtaining (see Aydemir and Skuterud 2008);

---

13 See, for example, Baker and Benjamin (1994); Bloom, Grenier, and Gunderson (1995); Grant (1999); McDonald and Worswick (1998); Schaafsma and Sweetman (2001); Frenette and Morrisette (2003); Bonikowska, Green, and Riddell (2008); Picot and Hou (2009); and Nadeau and Seckin (2010). Generally, the studies find larger declines in the 1990s than the 1980s and continuing through to 2005. Surveys of this literature can be found in Hum and Simpson (2004); Thompson and Worswick (2005); Reitz (2006 and 2007 a,b) and Hou and Picot (2010). The results reflect broadly similar patterns in the United States, as highlighted by Borjas (1985, 1995b) and Smith (2006), though with some interesting differences for highly educated immigrants — see Hou and Picot (2010).

- the countries in which the immigrant obtained the skills;
- the immigrant's ability to convert foreign-acquired skills to higher earnings in Canada — for example, by obtaining recognition of foreign credentials or permission to practise one's profession;
- the immigrant's facility in English or French, which aids in the effective use of skills in the labour market;
- the influence of Canada's immigration selection process on who gets into Canada for what skills;
- the degree of occupational matching between source-country and Canadian occupational distributions (see Goldmann, Sweetman, and Warman 2009);
- the possibility of discrimination and of employers' discounting foreign sources of human capital (whether training or work experience);
- macroeconomic conditions prevailing in Canada when the immigrant arrives; and
- the size of the returns to skills that are available elsewhere — highly educated workers might find they can do better in, say, the United States, the United Kingdom, or Australia — which could affect their choice to come to Canada or to remain here (see Bonikowska, Hou, and Picot 2008).

Ferrer and Riddell (2008), using Canadian census data, find that, over the 1981–2001 period, immigrants earned significantly lower returns to years of education and years of work experience than did Canadian-born workers (both men and women), with generally larger reductions in returns for immigrants who arrived after age 35 than for those who were younger on arrival. The authors conclude: "Differences between immigrants and the native born in the returns to human capital are evident for immigrants arriving as adults, but much less so for youth arrivals. This suggests that the human capital of immigrants who complete their education in Canada is not substantially discounted by the Canadian labour market, in contrast to the situation for immigrants who obtained their education before arrival" (213). Chiswick and Miller (2010) report similar results.

The interesting — indeed, policy relevant — question, then, is: what is driving these results? Green and Worswick (2002, 2010b) argue that immigrants share with young Canadian-born workers the characteristic of being recent entrants into the full-time labour market. For reasons not fully understood, young cohorts of workers in Canada over the past 25 years have seen their early career earnings slip by 15 to 20 percent compared with those of young workers a generation ago (Beaudry and Green 2000). From this perspective, Green and Worswick (2002) find that most of the slippage of immigrant initial earnings over the 1980s simply reflects the general decline of earnings of new entrants over this period, no matter who they were.

During the 1990s, however, other factors seem to be at work that are more specific to immigrants. For example, the earnings of immigrants tended to be more responsive to macroeconomic fluctuations and labour market weakness than those of more established workers (McDonald and Worswick

1997, 1998; Aydemir 2003). The first half of the 1990s was a period of labour market upheaval (the early 1990s recession and adjustment to the free trade agreements) and major public sector cutbacks to address government deficits. The major recession of the early 1990s was also the first in which the authorities maintained the relatively high rate of inflow of immigrants to Canada, rather than turn the tap down.

Many researchers, however, highlight the changing source-country composition of immigrants as a major contributor to their declining relative earnings. Many more immigrants now come from non-traditional source regions such as Asia and the Middle East, and far fewer of these arrivals are likely to be fluent in either English or French. The North American labour market may operate in a different way than new arrivals are used to, and their human capital skills may not be readily transferable to the highly organized, increasingly technological Canadian workplace. Immigrants who are relatively weak in English or French find it harder to learn to operate and communicate effectively in such an environment, and harder to reap the benefits of their home-country education. It is also possible that the presence of a larger number of visible minorities gives rise to labour market discrimination. More generally, many studies find that the change in source-country composition was the primary cause of the widening earnings gap, particularly over the 1980s and into the 1990s.[14] Aydemir and Skuterud (2005), for example, estimate that about one-third of the decline in immigrant earnings at time of arrival can be explained by the change in the source countries and language abilities of immigrants.

A more recent literature on this widening earnings gap highlights the growth of ethnic enclaves in major immigrant-receiving cities. Since 1980, the great majority of immigrants have settled in Toronto, Montreal, and Vancouver. The growing gentrification of neighbourhoods in the downtown cores of these cities — the traditional first place of settlement for immigrants — has pushed up housing costs there, forcing a growing fraction of immigrants to settle in suburban ethnic enclaves, many with growing degrees of poverty (Hou 2004). While such enclaves might provide many social and consumption benefits, in their relative isolation they also slow the process of economic adjustment and catch-up by limiting the incentives and opportunities for learning the local official language and dampening the development of a network of connections for job opportunities and work

---

14 On this issue, see Baker and Benjamin (1994); Hum and Simpson (1999); Chiswick and Miller (2001, 2008); Green and Worswick (2002); Aydemir and Skuterud (2005); Picot and Sweetman (2005); and Bonikowska, Green, and Riddell (2008).

arrangements (Boyd 2009). Warman (2007b), for example, finds a negative relationship between measures of ethnic segregation and earnings growth for both women and men in Canadian cities, and this relationship is particularly marked for better-educated immigrants.

Indeed, education is a key dimension of the deteriorating earnings gap between immigrants and non-immigrants. We have already seen that, since the 1990s, Canada's immigration system has brought in a large number of university graduates, who have had to compete with a growing number of domestic university graduates, thus reducing the premium to a university degree in Canada (Reitz 2007). Foreign-educated immigrants have significantly lower literary skills than Canadian-educated workers, which might inhibit their receiving the full benefit of their foreign-obtained training (Ferrer, Green, and Riddell 2006). Moreover, the quality of education varies substantially from one country of origin to another, and the shift of immigrants to "more foreign" sources since the 1980s has meant that more immigrants are arriving with education and training that are less attuned to, or up to date with, North American standards and ways of doing things. As a result, Canadian employers might find it harder to evaluate a person's foreign education and thereby discount its value, lowering the immigrant's returns on that education — though the extent of the gap between the returns to foreign versus Canadian education does not appear to have widened (McBride and Sweetman 2003; Aydemir and Skuterud 2005). Immigrants who are younger on arrival and who are more likely to complete their education in Canada seem to experience little or no discounting of their education in the labour market.

The shift of Canadian immigration policy in the mid-1990s toward increasing the share of the Economic Class and weighting formal education, especially a university degree, more heavily within the point system have successfully raised the education standards of arriving immigrants. Warman (2007a, 2010) finds, moreover, that, in stark contrast to the situation for permanent immigrants, *temporary* foreign workers have not experienced a discounting of their foreign human capital skills. Since the latter are largely employer selected, while the former are selected through the government-designated point system, this suggests that the form of the selection process to admit foreign workers — and particularly the source of information underlying it — has an important effect on immigrants' earnings outcomes upon arrival in Canada.[15]

15 Hawthorne (2008) notes that, since Australia changed its skilled immigrant selection procedure in the late 1990s, immigrants to that country over the past ten years have done much better in the labour market than have immigrants to Canada.

Another critical dimension of the deteriorating earnings gap between immigrants and non-immigrants, however, appears to be age and foreign work experience. Arriving immigrants who are older enter and compete in a labour market that already has an aging workforce. And again, the human capital skills they acquired in a quite different economy with perhaps different technological standards, organizational style, and language of operation may not be readily transferable to the Canadian workplace. The ongoing shift to employment in the services sector further highlights the importance of the need for effective communications skills, and increases the challenge immigrants from non-traditional source countries face as they seek to benefit from their home-country work experience.[16] Moreover, the returns to foreign experience also appear to have been deteriorating further since the 1980s and particularly during the 1990s[17] — an experience of non-English- or French-speaking, non-European immigrants, and largely related to the changing source-country composition of immigrants (see Green and Worswick 2010a). Major restructuring of the Canadian economy in the early and mid-1990s to accommodate the advent of the Canada-US and North American Free Trade Agreements may have made immigrant adjustment more difficult. As in the case of the valuation of foreign education, the general shift to a more knowledge-based, services-sector-oriented economy where language fluency plays a more critical role may have further reduced the valuation of foreign work experience (Reitz 2001, 2005), especially for those from non-traditional source countries. Immigrants who are older on arrival in fact experience this deterioration more than younger arrivals with less foreign work experience, as they may be less adaptable to new workplace methods and viewed by employers as more costly to support on the job while they learn and adapt.

During the early 2000s, however, Picot and Hou (2009) and Hou and Picot (2010) argue that the decline in immigrants' relative earnings was very much concentrated in the information technology (IT)-related occupations following the dot-com bust of the early 2000s since a large number of the highly educated immigrants arriving in the 1990s were working in this field.

More generally, Green and Worswick (2010a) conclude:

> We can break the movements in immigrant entry earnings into three periods. In the 1980s, a substantial decline in these earnings was most strongly related to the fact that earnings were declining for all new labour market entrants, immigrants and non-immigrants. Thus, movements in the macro economy affecting all new workers were the

---

16 See Schaafsma and Sweetman (2001); Aydemir and Skuterud (2005); Ferrer and Riddell (2008); and Skuterud and Su (2009).

17 See Green and Worswick (2002); Aydemir and Skuterud (2005); and Skuterud and Su (2009).

dominant force shaping the experience of new immigrants. In the 1990s, these macro effects continued to be important, but the single most important factor in the on-going decline in immigrant earnings was the virtual eradication of returns to foreign experience. By the mid-1990s, an immigrant just out of school and another immigrant with the same level of schooling but 20 years of experience outside of Canada could expect to have the same average entry earnings in Canada. This occurred at a time when shifts in immigration policy resulted in a strong increase in the average education level of new immigrants. Without these shifts, average entry earnings would have fallen a further 20 percent in the 1990s. On the other hand, in the early 2000s (the third period)… highly educated immigrants were particularly negatively affected by the information technology bust…[and] returns to foreign acquired experience continued to be low. (107)

Hou (2010), however, is less pessimistic:

By focusing the research on three distinct time periods, and observing the changing effects of major explanatory factors, the research points to a less pessimistic picture about the labour market performance of Canada's recent immigrants in the recent past. The largest increase in the gap was observed during the 1980s, driven largely by compositional shifts, most of which abated during the 1990s, and certainly by the 2000s. The shifts in immigrant source regions and language ability have stabilized and may not negatively affect trends in immigrants' earnings gap in the near future, barring some possible significant change in immigration patterns….The reason for the expanding earnings gap is unique in the early 2000s when the downturn of a single industrial sector (IT) affected a substantial share of recent immigrants. A similar event may not be repeated, although it remains to be seen what effects the recent recession of 2008–09 had on immigrants' relative earnings. (3)

Clearly, the role of skills has been an important factor in the changing outcomes for earnings of arriving immigrants to Canada. It makes sense to pursue an examination of how policy changes have had an effect on these skill levels of arriving immigrants and hence on their earnings levels – the subject of the next chapter.

Chapter 6

The Effects of Policy Levers on Immigrants' Earnings

In this chapter, we address the effects of key policy lever changes on the average earnings of new immigrants to Canada. The analysis makes use of the results in Chapter 4, which looked at the effects of changes in policy levers on the skills characteristics of landing immigrants, and Chapter 5, which examined the effects of these characteristics on the expected entry or early levels of earnings of arriving immigrants. Here, we link the two and put a dollar value on the effects of changes to key immigration policy levers.

In so doing, we build an empirical framework for estimating such effects based on current best-practice empirical results from the available research literature. This then gives us a tool or criterion for evaluating how well immigrants are doing in the Canadian labour market. The objective of the exercise is to improve the ability to choose the immigration approaches that work better. For example, we can illustrate the estimated effect of changes in the overall level of immigration (LOM) on average (log) earnings levels of immigrants (LYE) through the former's effect on average education levels of landing immigrants (ED) as:

$$\text{Effect (LOM on ED)} \times \text{Effect (ED on LYE)} \longrightarrow \text{Effect (LOM on LYE)}_{\text{ED}}.$$

We obviously should acknowledge that improving immigrant earnings is not the only goal of immigration policy, but since our particular focus in this book is on the labour market outcomes of skilled immigrants in the Economic Class of immigrants, a conventional and readily available indicator of labour market performance is earnings. Moreover, it is a measure that lends itself to quantitative analysis and ready comparison with established studies in the labour market literature.

Here, we look at the effects on *entry earnings* or on the average earnings of immigrants in the first full calendar year after their arrival. This approach is in contrast to looking at the long-run or career earnings of immigrants after earnings growth and labour market adjustments take place that typically narrow the earnings gap between immigrants and non-immigrants. That perspective is certainly interesting, and the subject of a major research literature, but to incorporate it into our framework would lengthen and complicate the study unnecessarily. In any event, entry earnings are of interest in their own right, for several reasons. They are straightforward in concept and an intuitive metric for evaluating economic well-being. Initial low earnings might be of greater concern to politicians and analysts as an indicator of the hardship new arrivals face than earnings after immigrants have adjusted more to the Canadian environment. As well, as we have seen, immigration policy levers have direct effects on the skills characteristics of incoming immigrants, and the link between these characteristics and immigrants' subsequent earnings is well established. Also, to the extent that longer-run economic outcomes depend on the initial economic status and skills characteristics of arriving immigrants, the level of entry earnings can affect their eventual labour market outcomes and economic well-being in their adopted country. Indeed, studies of immigrants' career earnings profiles do not find major differences between the entry and career earnings outcomes of immigrants (Green and Worswick 2004, 2010a).

In the analysis of this section, we link the two concepts of age at landing (from Chapter 4) with the human capital concept of the work experience effect on workers' earnings (from Chapter 5). The rationale for lower age as a desirable "skill" is that it proxies the greater adaptability, flexibility, and rapid ability to learn of youth in a new labour market environment. We represent the market value of this adaptability effect as what the new worker would earn on average from a year in the Canadian labour market — the human capital work experience effect estimates reviewed in Chapter 5. And just as the work experience effect decreases for older workers, so also does the adaptability effect.

Any set of estimates cannot be totally comprehensive, and is based on some restrictive assumptions, so estimation results have to be qualified or viewed in context. First, we look only at total annual earnings of immigrants, and do not break down the earnings effects into components operating through wage rates, employment rates, and average hours worked. This approach would have required a more complex and structured analysis than we have undertaken, but our framework could be extended to accommodate it. Second, we do not look at the effects of immigration on the employment, wages, and earnings of workers in the labour market already resident in Canada. There is a substantial literature on this important topic,[1] but the analytical framework to best address this topic is quite different from the current framework and involves general equilibrium feedback effects — this would require a major study in its own right, and the conclusions depend very much upon some quite technical assumptions that the analytical literature is still in the process of sorting out. We also do not look at the net economic benefits to the economy as a whole from continuing immigration (see Borjas 1995a), as this, too, would require a quite different form of analysis, nor would it provide a fiscal cost-benefit analysis of immigration for public budgets (see Akbari 1989, 1995; Bonin 2006). Third, we look only at the average effects on immigrants' earnings, not at the distribution or inequality of earnings outcomes or the incidence of low-income among immigrants and their families. These would require quite separate studies. Fourth, the analysis of point system weight effects does not treat Quebec separately from the rest of the country, as we make use of only the federal point system weight schedule for simplicity. Finally, we should emphasize that an estimated effect of some policy lever does not mean that a policy is being undertaken efficiently or could not be done better — it is simply an estimate of the effect of a particular policy lever. Again, when we use the term Economic Class immigrants, we refer to immigrants arriving under the Federal Skilled Worker Program.

Calculating the Effects of Policy Lever Changes on the Earnings of Arriving Immigrants

Here, we outline the construction of the calculations of how changes in the major immigration policy levers with respect to the education, age, and degree of language fluency (in either English or French) of arriving immigrants affect their earnings. For more details on the calculations, see Appendix C, which examines the effects of arriving immigrants' skills characteristics on their entry earnings, and Appendix D, which combines the results in Appendixes B and C to calculate policy lever effects on entry earnings levels through their effects on immigrants' average skills characteristics.

The Effects of Changing the Overall Level of Immigration

Consider, first, the effect of changes in the overall level of immigration (LOM). The effect operates through the three skills channels of education, age,

---

1 See, for example, Johnson (1980); Borjas (2003); Dustmann, Hatton, and Preston (2005); Wanner (2006); Dustmann, Glitz, and Frattini (2008); and Card (2009).

and language fluency of the landing immigrants. From Appendix Table A-1, one takes that

Effect (LOM on ED) = −.00310,

where "Effect (LOM on ED)" is shorthand for the partial derivative of LOM on the dependent variable ED in an education level regression equation in Table A-1. So the effect of raising the level of immigration by 100,000 is −.31 years, or a reduction of about a third of a year of education.[2] From Appendix Table A-4, an additional year of education can be calculated as raising men's earnings by 8.17 percent; Aydemir and Skuterud (2005) provide a corresponding estimate for women of 10.22 percent. But these estimates of returns to years of education are essentially relevant to Canadian-born workers, who typically do not get their education abroad. The returns to education for immigrants are generally estimated to be less. Again, Aydemir and Skuterud (2005) estimate the foreign discounts for returns to years of education to be 21.1 percent for men and 33.5 percent for women. For male immigrants, then, the return to years of education is

Effect (ED on LYE) = .0817[1 − .211] = .0645,

where LYE is the log of workers' annual earnings. For women immigrants, this comes to .1022 [1 − .335] = .0680. Consequently, the estimated effect through education for men of increasing the total level of immigration by 100,000 is

$$\text{Effect (LOM on LYE)}_{ED} = \text{Effect (LOM on ED)} \times \text{Effect (ED on LYE)}$$
$$= (-.31) \times (.0645) = -.0200,$$

or a decrease in entry earnings of male immigrants of about 2.0 percent. The corresponding calculation for female immigrants yields an estimated reduction in earnings of 2.1 percent.[3]

---

2 The selection of 100,000 as the increase in the overall level of immigration is an arbitrary number that readily illustrates the calculations involved and is within the realm of past changes. Perhaps a more politically realistic possible change nowadays would be 50,000. Because of the (linear) nature of the calculation of the LOM effects, the results for a 50,000 change in immigration levels are exactly half those reported for a 100,000 change.

3 These calculations are based on the assumption that the gender proportions of an increase in LOM are the same as for the level of immigration as a whole.

But changes in LOM also operate through age effects. From Appendix Table A-2,

Effect (LOM on AGE) = −.00290,

so that raising the level of immigration by 100,000 reduces the average age of arriving immigrants by .29 years. Now, for given levels of education, differences in age for men essentially correspond to differences in years of work experience, so the age effect in Table A-4 corresponds to the experience effect:

Effect (EXP on LYE) = .034 − .00114EXP.

At an average age of about 30 and average years of education of about 12, arriving immigrants average about 12 years of work experience. So the experience effect, or return to a year of work experience, can be evaluated as .020, or 2.0 percent higher earnings. By comparison, Ferrer and Riddell (2008) find that the corresponding return to work experience for Canadian-born women is 2.06 percent. They also find that the returns on foreign work experience are discounted by 76.4 percent for men and by 88.3 percent for women. So, for immigrant women,

Effect (EXP on LYE) = .0206[1 − .883] = .00241,

while for immigrant men, .0203 [1 − .764] = .00479. Consequently, the estimated effect operating through age at the time of immigrant women's arrival of increasing the total level of immigration by 100,000 is

Effect (LOM on LYE)$_{AGE}$ = Effect (LOM on AGE) × Effect (EXP on LYE) = (−.29) × (.00241) = −.000699,

or a decrease in the entry earnings of female immigrants of about 0.07 percent. A similar calculation for male immigrants yields an estimated reduction in earnings of 0.14 percent.

In addition, however, changing the total level of immigration also has an effect on the average degree of language fluency of arriving immigrants. From Appendix Table A-3,

Effect (LOM on PLF) = −.00011,

so that raising the level of immigration by 100,000 reduces the proportion of arriving immigrants who are fluent in either English or French (PLF) by

0.011, or 1.1 percentage points. But greater literacy scores have been found to have a strong effect on a worker's earnings. Using several estimates of literacy effects on earnings for immigrants in Canada from Bonikowska, Green, and Riddell (2008), we can calculate that

Effect (PLF on LYE) = 1.187,

for immigrant men and, correspondingly, 1.108 for immigrant women. Combining these results,

Effect $(LOM \text{ on } LYE)_{LF}$ = Effect (LOM on PLF) × Effect (PLF on LYE)
= (−.00011) × (1.187) = −.0001306,

for men, and −.0001219 for women. That is, increasing the total level of immigration by 100,000 reduces immigrant men's average earnings by .013, or 1.3 percent, and immigrant women's earnings by 1.2 percent.

The combined effect, then, of increasing the overall level of immigration operates through all three skills channels, so that the combined effect is the sum of the three separate effects:

Effect (LOM on LYE) = Effect $(LOM \text{ on } LYE)_{ED}$ + Effect (LOM on LYE)$_{AGE}$ + Effect (LOM on LYE)$_{LF}$.

For women, this comes to −.0339 (or a 3.39 percent reduction in entry earnings levels), and for men it is estimated as −.0345 (or a 3.45 percent reduction). Thus, the education channel comes through as the strongest component, the age or experience channel as the weakest, and the language fluency channel as about 60 percent of the strength of the education channel.

The Effects of Changing the Economic Class Share of Immigration

Next, we consider the effects of changing the share of immigrants entering under the Economic Class (ECS). Again, changing ECS operates through three channels: its effect on average education levels, on average age at landing, and on the average proportion that is fluent in either English or French. The effect of changes in ECS on immigrants' entry earnings operating through the average years-of-education channel is

Effect $(ECS \text{ on } LYE)_{ED}$ = Effect (ECS on ED) × Effect (ED on LYE).

The first term in the expression is calculated from Appendix Table A-1 as .0259. The second term was calculated above as .0645 for men and .0680 for women. Consequently, the estimated effect through education of raising the Economic Class share of immigration by, say, 10 percentage points is to increase average earnings of landing immigrants by (.0259) × (.0645) × 10 = .01671, or by 1.7 percent for men and 1.8 percent for women.

But changing the Economic Class share of immigration also affects the average age of arriving immigrants and hence their amount of work experience and earnings through the average age-at-arrival channel:

$$\text{Effect (ECS on LYE)}_{AGE} = \text{Effect (ECS on AGE)} \times \text{Effect (EXP on LYE)}.$$

Once again, the first term in the expression is calculated from the regression results in Appendix Table A-2 as −.0273, and the second term was calculated above as .00479 for men and .00241 for women. Consequently, the estimated effect of increasing the Economic Class share, again by 10 percentage points, through its effect on the average age of arriving immigrants is to reduce the average earnings of landing immigrants by (−.0273) × (.00479) × 10 = -.00131, or by about 0.13 percent for men and 0.07 percent for women.

The third channel through which changes in the Economic Class share of immigration affect the earnings of arriving immigrants is through their average degree of language fluency:

$$\text{Effect (ECS on LYE)}_{LF} = \text{Effect (ECS on PLF)} \times \text{Effect (PLF on LYE)},$$

where PLF is the proportion of arriving immigrants that is fluent in either English or French. Again, the first term can be calculated from Appendix Table A-3 as .005065, and the second term was calculated above as 1.187 for men and 1.108 for women. Thus, combining these two effects, a 10 percentage point increase in the Economic Class share of immigration is estimated to raise the average earnings levels of arriving immigrants by (.005065) × (1.187) × 10 = .06012, or by about 6.0 percent for males, and by .05612 (5.6 percent) for females.

The combined effect of increasing the Economic Class share of immigration on earnings levels or on arriving immigrants operating through these three skills channels is then the sum of the three separate effects:

$$\text{Effect (ECS on LYE)} = \text{Effect (ECS on LYE)}_{ED} + \text{Effect (ECS on LYE)}_{AGE} + \text{Effect (ECS on LYE)}_{LF}.$$

For women, this comes to .0730, or a 7.3 percent increase in earnings; for men, this is .0755, or about a 7.5 percent rise in earnings. For both groups, the language fluency channel component is by far the largest, the age or experience channel is very minor, and the education channel lies in between.

The Effect of Changing Skills Weights in the Point System for Economic Class Immigrants

The effects on the entry earnings of arriving immigrants of changing the point system's weights on specific skills are more straightforward to calculate. The relevant group these effects operate on now is just the principal applicants — specifically, those directly evaluated by the point system arriving in the Economic Class.[4] These effects also operate through only one channel each. For example, changing the maximum points for years of education operates just through the average years of education of arriving immigrants, and changing the maximum points for age operates just through the average age on arrival. If PSW_{ED} is the point system weight for years of education, then,

$$\text{Effect } (PSW_{ED} \text{ on LYE}) = \text{Effect } (PSW_{ED} \text{ on ED}) \times \text{Effect } (ED \text{ on LYE}),$$

where the first term in the expression is taken from the estimates in Appendix Table A-1; the second term was calculated above. In this calculation, we estimate that the effect of increasing the point system's maximum weight for years of education by 10 percentage points is to increase the entry earnings of male principal applicants by .0228, or about 2.3 percent. For female principal applicants, the effect raises entry earnings by .0240, or about 2.4 percent.

Similarly, if PSW_{AGE} is the weight given for age upon the principal applicant's arrival, then,

$$\text{Effect } (PSW_{AGE} \text{ on LYE}) = \text{Effect } (PSW_{AGE} \text{ on AGE}) \times \text{Effect } (EXP \text{ on LYE}),$$

where the first term comes from Appendix Table A-2 and the second was also calculated above. In this case, increasing the maximum weight given for age at arrival by 10 percentage points *decreases* their average entry earnings levels by 0.08 percent. For female principal applicants, the result is a 0.04 percent fall in average earnings. Both these effects, however, are negligible.

---

4 The results we find for principal applicants are actually likely to apply more broadly among Economic Class immigrants because the labour market skills of spouses are generally positively correlated through assortive marriage patterns (Hou and Myles, 2007; Pencavel, 1998).

Finally, if PSW_{LF} is the point system weight awarded for language fluency (in either English or French) on the part of the principal applicant, then,

$$\text{Effect } (PSW_{LF} \text{ on LYE}) = \text{Effect } (PSW_{LF} \text{ on PLF}) \times \text{Effect (PLF on LYE)}.$$

Again, the first term in this expression comes from Appendix Table A-3, and the second term was calculated above. The estimated effect, then, of increasing the maximum weight given to language fluency by 10 percentage points is to increase average entry earnings by about 1.1 percent for male principal applicants and by about 1.0 percent for female principal applicants.[5]

A Discussion of the Estimates

The first set of results from these calculations is summarized in Table 16, which shows the percentage changes in the entry earnings of landing immigrants arising from the various policy lever changes considered above. The first result is an increase in the total level of immigration by 100,000 landings per year. The second is an increase in the Economic Class share by 10 percentage points. The last three results are increases by 10 percentage points in the maximum points allocated within the point system schedule to either years of education, age on arrival, or degree of language fluency. The results are broken down by males and females and by the channels through which the policy lever effects operate.

Turn first to the first column and bottom rows of Table 16, total effects, which show that increasing the total level of immigration by 100,000 a year (holding the immigration class mix constant) reduces the entry earnings levels of landing immigrants by 3.39 to 3.45 percent as the larger inflow reduces the marginal skills levels of arrivals. On the other hand, as the second column shows, raising the Economic Class share of immigration by 10 percentage points (for a given total level of immigration) raises the average entry earnings levels of incoming immigrants by 7.30 to 7.55 percent, as the arrival of more highly skilled workers increases immigrants' average earnings levels. Increasing the (maximum) weight on a given skill dimension within the point system indeed has the effect of raising earnings levels of arriving principal applicants through education and language fluency. Increasing the point system weight on education by 10 percentage points raises principal applicants' average

---

5 It would not be a good use of the analytical framework developed in this study to estimate the effects of the complete elimination of points in some category of the point system. All our calculations are based on marginal or incremental changes since they involve applying derivatives to various skills-outcome and earnings equations. The complete elimination of points in some category indeed would be interesting to examine, but it is beyond the practical applicability of the current approach.

Table 16: Effects of Policy Lever Changes on Immigrants' Average Entry Earnings, by Skill Channel and Sex

	LOM	ECS	Combined	PSW_{ED}	PSW_{AGE}	PSW_{LF}
			Policy Lever			
			(percentage change)			
Effects via ED						
Males	−2.00	1.67	−0.10	2.28	/	/
Females	−2.11	1.76	−0.10	2.40	/	/
Effects via AGE						
Males	−0.14	−0.13	−0.29	/	−0.082	/
Females	−0.07	−0.07	−0.15	/	−0.038	/
Effects via PLF						
Males	−1.31	6.01	5.54	/	/	1.08
Females	−1.22	5.61	5.18	/	/	1.01
Total Effects						
Males	−3.45	7.55	5.16	2.28	−0.082	1.08
Females	−3.39	7.30	4.92	2.40	−0.038	1.01

Notes:
LOM = Level of Immigration; ECS = Education Class Share; PSW = Point System Weight; ED = Education; AGE = Age; PLF = proportion with host-country language fluency.

The first column refers to an increase in the total level of immigration by 100,000 immigrants per year.
The second column refers to an increase in the Economic Class share by 10 percentage points.
The third column refers to the effect of increasing the total inflow of immigrants by 100,000 per year solely by raising the Economic Class numbers.
The fourth column refers to an increase in the maximum point system weight allocated to years of education by 10 percentage points.
The fifth column refers to an increase in the maximum point system weight allocated to age by 10 percentage points.
The last column refers to an increase in the maximum point system weight allocated to language fluency by 10 percentage points.
Source: Authors' calculations.

earnings levels by 2.28 to 2.40 percent. And raising the weight on language fluency by 10 percentage points increases principal applicants' average earnings by 1.01 to 1.08 percent. The effect of raising the weight on the age of the principal applicant, however, is essentially negligible. The effects in general differ little between males and females.

Thus, the policy lever of changing the Economic Class share of the immigration inflow is very strong, and raising this share works in the direction of higher average earnings by arriving immigrants. Raising the overall level of immigration (holding the immigrant class mix constant) has a moderately strong effect, but works in the direction of reducing average starting earnings of new arrivals. As for the point system weight levers, that on education has quite a strong effect, that on language fluency a moderate effect, and that on age an extremely weak effect.

In terms of the strengths of the different skills channels, education and language fluency are by far the strongest, while the age channel is again extremely weak. The strength of the former two channels reflects both that they are relatively amenable to policy change and that they have very strong effects on workers' earnings in the Canadian labour market.

The earnings changes shown in Table 16 might be easier to grasp if expressed in actual dollar terms. To do this, we draw on Frenette and Morrisette (2003, 16), who estimate the average earnings in 2000 of immigrants who arrived over the 1995–99 period as $26,793 for women and $37,909 for men (in then current dollars). We multiply these up by the rate of consumer price index inflation to mid-2008[6] to get corresponding figures of $32,286 for women and $45,680 for men. We then multiply all the percentage changes in Table 16 by these respective 2008 estimated earnings levels, and show the results in Table 17. The total effect of increasing new arrivals by 100,000 a year is to reduce average entry earnings levels by between $1,098 and $1,576. The corresponding effect of increasing the Economic Class share of immigration (holding the total inflow level constant) by 10 percentage points is to increase average entry earnings levels by $2, 357 to $3,449. A 10 percentage point rise in the education points corresponds to principal applicants' average earnings levels going up by between $775 and $1,041, and a corresponding rise in language fluency points raises principal applicants' earnings on average by between $326 and $493. The difference in the size of the effects between males and females is enhanced because of differences in their average levels of earnings in the Canadian labour market.

These effects are fairly substantial. While they refer to effects only on the entry earnings of landing immigrants, if they were to persist over a career that averages 30 years in length in Canada, the long-run effects on earnings would be quite significant indeed.

Now consider two extensions of the above analysis. In the first, we combine the effects in the first two columns in Tables 16 and 17 by increasing the immigration rate by 100,000 per year, with the increase consisting solely of those in the Economic Class; the results are shown in the third column of these tables.[7] Since most of the two effects are of opposite sign, the positive ECS effects counter the negative LOM effects. The result is a net increase in

---

6 The inflation adjustment over this period, 20.5 percent, is from Statistics Canada (2008a, 52).

7 Since the Economic Class accounts for about 60 percent of total immigration, if the initial number of landing immigrants is 250,000 a year, then the initial number in the Economic Class immigrants is 150,000. An increase of 100,000 Economic Class immigrants corresponds both to the total level of immigration going up from 250,000 to 350,000 and to the Economic Class share rising from 60 percent to 71.4 percent [(150 + 100)/(250 + 100)], or by 11.4 percentage points. The combined effect can then be readily calculated as the sum of (i) the figures in column 1 of Tables 16 and 17; and (ii) 1.14 times the figures in column 2 of the tables.

Table 17: Dollar-Value Effects of Policy Lever Changes on Immigrants' Average Entry Earnings, by Skill Channel and Sex

	LOM	ECS	Policy Lever Combined (change in 2008 dollars)	PSW_{ED}	PSW_{AGE}	PSW_{LF}
Effects via ED						
Males	−913.6	762.9	−43.9	1,041.5	/	/
Females	−681.2	568.2	−33.4	774.9	/	/
Effects via AGE						
Males	−64.0	−59.4	−131.7	/	−37.5	/
Females	−22.6	−22.6	−48.4	/	−12.3	/
Effects via PLF						
Males	−598.4	2,745.4	2,531.4	/	/	493.3
Females	−393.9	1,811.2	1,670.9	/	/	326.1
Total Effects						
Males	−1,576.0	3,448.9	2,355.8	1,041.5	−37.5	493.3
Females	−1,097.7	2,356.8	1,589.1	774.9	−12.3	326.1

Notes:
LOM = Level of Immigration; ECS = Education Class Share; PSW = Point System Weight; ED = Education; AGE = Age; PLF = Proportion with host-country language fluency.

The first column refers to an increase in the total level of immigration by 100,000 immigrants per year.
The second column refers to an increase in the Economic Class share by 10 percentage points.
The third column refers to the effect of increasing the total inflow of immigrants by 100,000 per year solely by raising the Economic Class numbers.
The fourth column refers to an increase in the maximum point system weight allocated to years of education by 10 percentage points.
The fifth column refers to an increase in the maximum point system weight allocated to age by 10 percentage points.
The last column refers to an increase in the maximum point system weight allocated to language fluency by 10 percentage points.
Source: Authors' calculations.

the average entry earnings of immigrant males of 5.2 percent (or $2,356) and in the earnings of females of 4.9 percent ($1,589), as the Economics-Class-share effect clearly dominates the level-of-immigration effect, essentially because of the very strong impact of language fluency associated with bringing in more Economic Class immigrants.

The second extension further strengthens the education-points effect. In August 1993, Citizenship and Immigration Canada increased the maximum points allocated to education in the point system schedule from 12 to 16, with the extra 4 points to be awarded for completion of a bachelor's degree at a university (see McWhinney 1998, 5, 33). We accommodated this policy change in the analysis in Chapter 4 by adding to the education outcome regression in Appendix Table A-1 a dummy indicator variable for 1993 or later (henceforth D93).[8] The coefficient on this term for principal applicants is 0.4150 and is highly statistically significant. Its implication for the entry earnings effects for arriving immigrants can be calculated as

$$\text{Effect (D93 on LYE)} = \text{Effect (D93 on ED)} \times \text{Effect (ED on LYE)}$$
$$= (.4150) \times (.0645) = .02677,$$

for male immigrants and .02822 for female immigrants. That is, this separate change is estimated to have increased the average entry earnings of arriving principal applicants by 2.7 to 2.8 percent, quite separate from the previously calculated years-of-education effect shown in the top panel, fourth row, of Tables 16 and 17. This is really quite significant, and provides strong rationale for increasing the weight in the point system on educational attainment as an important skill dimension in the labour market. This is also consistent with Ferrer and Riddell's (2008) finding of strong earnings benefits for immigrants who complete educational programs. In dollar terms, the increases are estimated to have been $1,224 for males and $910 for females.

Would it have been a better use of education-related points simply to add these points to those already awarded to years of education? Doing so would have increased such points by 5.97 percentage points (relative to the pass mark of 67 points). With the figures for PSW_{ED} in Tables 16 and 17 for a 10 percentage point increase in the weight on ED, we calculate the PSW_{ED} effects of the 5.97 point increase would have been to increase average entry earnings levels of males by $622 and of females by $463, substantially less than the increase from putting the extra points on having completed a degree. Consequently, the 1993 move to increase the weight on education in the point system appears to have been quite sensible.

Business cycle effects — quite apart from the broad policy environment — also can have a strong impact on the skills levels of arriving immigrants. Since skills map into earnings, it is worth investigating how the average earnings levels of arriving immigrants are affected by the general health of the economy as measured by the unemployment rate prevailing on arrival. And since the United States can be viewed as an alternative potential destination of immigrants to Canada, we include the effects of both the Canadian and the US unemployment rates. The relative strength of business cycle effects in the two countries, as represented by their respective unemployment rates, on the skills levels of immigrants landing in Canada were presented in Table

---

8 While the use of a time-shift dummy variable to capture the effect of a policy change at a particular time is a common technique, the dummy also might pick up the effects of other ongoing changes initiated at the same time.

Table 18: Effects of Changes in Canadian and US Unemployment Rates on Average Entry Earnings of Principal Applicants, by Skill Channel and Sex

	Canadian Unemployment Rate	US Unemployment Rate	Combined Recession Effect
		(% change in earnings)	
Effects via Education			
Males	−1.87	3.79	5.39
Females	−1.97	3.99	5.68
Effects via Age			
Males	0.74	−0.56	−0.38
Females	0.37	−0.28	−0.19
Effects via PLF			
Males	15.25	−15.37	−14.97
Females	14.23	−14.34	−13.97
Total Effects			
Males	14.12	−12.14	−9.96
Females	12.63	−10.63	−8.48
Total Effects		*(change in 2008 dollars)*	
Males	6,450	−5,546	−4,550
Females	4,078	−3,432	−2,738

Notes:
Figures in columns 1 and 2 refer to increases in either the Canadian or US unemployment rate by 3 percentage points; see the detailed calculation in Appendix B.
Figures in column 3 refer to the combined effect of the Canadian unemployment rate's going up by 2.7 percentage points (from January 2008 to August 2009) and the US rate's rising by 5.6 percentage points (from 2007 to the third quarter of 2009). Both changes are from the pre-recession unemployment rate low to the peak-recession unemployment rate high.
The dollar values in the bottom panel are calculated by multiplying the total effects in proportional terms by 2008 estimated mean annual earnings of arriving immigrants of $45,680 for males and $32,286 for females.
Source: Authors' calculations.

15 in Chapter 4. Following the calculations detailed in Appendix B, we can now convert these effects on skills levels to their corresponding effects on the average earnings levels of landing principal applicant immigrants; see Table 18.

The first two columns of Table 18 show the percentage changes in the average entry earnings of principal applicants of a 3 percentage point increase in respective unemployment rates via the three skills channels, along with the resulting total change, with the first column showing the results for Canada and the second column the results for the United States. Note, first, the opposite signs of the effects of Canadian and US unemployment rates on the earnings of arriving immigrants and the very substantial magnitudes of these business cycle effects — a 3 percentage point change in unemployment rates results in a 10 to 14 percent change in earnings. Note also the leading role played by language fluency, which is both amenable to the immigrant selection process and has an important effect on work opportunities in the Canadian labour market. The education channel has a moderate effect, and it is more sensitive to changes in the US unemployment rate than the Canadian rate. Once again, the contribution of the age channel is negligible.

The third column in Table 18 shows the results of a simulation of the consequences of the recent major economic recession in North America on the entry earnings of arriving immigrants. From January 2008 to August 2009, the Canadian unemployment rate rose by 2.7 percentage points, while the US rate rose by 5.6 percentage points between 2007 and the third quarter of 2009.[9] Combining these two sets of unemployment rate changes yields the "combined recession effect" in the third column of Table 18.[10] The results show that the recession had a major negative effect on the average entry earnings levels of arriving principal applicant immigrants (indeed, for arriving immigrants as a whole[11]), reducing them by about 8 to 10 percent. For females, this represented a decline of more than $2,700 in their 2008 earnings levels; for males, the drop was an estimated $4,550. These declines are quite substantial indeed, both in their own right and relative to the policy lever outcomes discussed earlier. Also, while the average education level of arriving immigrants is expected to go up as many highly educated workers choose Canada over the United States because of the relatively stronger US downturn, the average language fluency skills of arrivals are estimated to decline strongly as immigration numbers are kept up, more than countering the beneficial education effect.

The Effects of Selected Policy Changes on Immigrants' Earnings

We can now use the general approach set out in Chapters 4 and 5 and the specific results from earlier in this chapter to estimate the effects on immigrants' average entry earnings levels of several alternative immigration policy changes, both tried and untried. Indeed, a key contribution of this volume, we believe, is that our direct estimates of the earnings implications of various policy alternatives can serve as a basis for evaluating those changes.

---

9 *Canadian Economic Observer* (February 2010), pp. 18, 71. In each case, the change was measured from the pre-recession unemployment rate low to the recession unemployment rate peak.

10 These figures are calculated by taking (2.7/3.0) times the results in column one of Table 18 and (5.6/3.0) times the results in column two and summing them.

11 See the coefficient signs on the Canadian and US unemployment rates in the first columns of regression results in Appendix Tables A-1 to A-3.

Table 19: Effects of Increasing Annual Immigration Inflow to 1 percent of the Population on Average Entry Earnings of Landing Immigrants, by Skill Channel and Sex				
		Skill Channel		
	Education	Age	Language Fluency	Total
		(proportional change)		
Males	−.0170	−.0012	−.0111	−.0293
Females	−.0179	−.0006	−.0104	−.0289

Source: Authors' calculations.

Raising the Annual Immigration Rate to 1 Percent of the Population

It has been suggested — particularly by those who view immigration as a policy tool to enhance Canada's demographic structure — that the annual immigration rate should be increased to 1 percent of the Canadian population. With a current population of about 33.5 million, this would mean raising annual immigration from a base of about 250,000 by an additional 85,000. All three skills channels through which this change would operate would be affected negatively, as shown by the immigration inflow coefficients in the first column of Appendix Tables A-1 through A-3. The proportional effects on average entry earnings through the various skills channels, shown in Table 19, imply a reduction of 2.93 percent ($1,337) for males and 2.89 percent ($932) for females.

Increasing the Economic Class Share of Immigration

We have already seen that changing the proportion of immigrants entering in the Economic Class is expected to have a substantial effect on the average skills levels of arrivals and hence on their average entry earnings levels. Did this, in fact, happen when the Economic Class share was increased from 35 percent of total immigration in the early 1980s to about 60 percent in 2000? Our results reveal, in Table 20, that the effect on earnings was substantial and occurred largely through the education and language fluency channels. The corresponding increase in average entry earnings for male immigrants was 18.9 percent (or $8,624, based on a mean earnings level of $45,680 in 2008) and for females 18.3 percent (or $5,898, based on a mean earnings level of $32,286). These large numbers might be surprising in light of the evidence that immigrant average earnings did not keep up with those of non-immigrants

Table 20: Effects of Increasing the Economic Class Share of Total Immigration from 35 percent to 60 percent on Average Entry Earnings of Landing Immigrants, by Skill Channel and Sex

| | | Skill Channel | | |
| | Education | Age | Language Fluency | Total |
		(proportional change)		
Males	.0418	−.0033	.1503	.1888
Females	.0440	−.0016	.1403	.1827

Source: Authors' calculations.

over this period. What these results indicate, however, is that the immigrant earnings gap would have been substantially worse if immigration policy had not increased the role of skills in assessing admissions to Canada.[12] Raising the average skills levels of landing immigrants over the past thirty years has certainly increased their average earnings levels.

A related question is how entry earnings would respond to major changes to the Economic Class's current 60 percent share of total immigrants — say, an increase to 80 percent or a decrease to 50 percent. As Table 21 shows, increasing the share by 20 percentage points is estimated to raise average entry earnings levels by about 15 percent, while decreasing the share by 10 percentage points reduces earnings by half that amount, or about 7.5 percent. Again, these numbers are quite substantial. As we have already seen, the Economic Class share is an effective policy tool, but since any such major change likely would be spread over several years of adjustment, the change might not seem so noticeable.

It may be the case, though, that setting the Economic Class share too high risks reducing the demand on the part of such immigrants to choose Canada, since many may wish to sponsor other family members such as parents and siblings and may apply elsewhere if they feel there is little prospect of being able to do so.

Restructuring the Points Given for Age Asymmetrically

Earlier, we found that points for age on arrival have a very weak effect on the average entry earnings of immigrants. In part, this reflects the symmetric way

---

12 The other part of the problem of the widening immigrant earnings gap is that it is averaged over the stock of all immigrants (not just the inflow of recently landed immigrants) and hence reflects the difficulties immigrants face in the labour market adjustment process following their arrival.

Table 21: Effects of Changing the Economic Class Share of Total Immigration on Average Entry Earnings of Landing Immigrants, by Sex

| | Change in Economic Class Share | | | |
| | Increase to 80% | | Decrease to 50% | |
	(% change)	($ change)	(% change)	($ change)
Males	+15.1	+6,897.8	−7.55	−3,448.9
Females	+14.6	+4,713.6	−7.30	−2,356.8

Source: Authors' calculations.

that age points are allocated within the Canadian point system. A maximum of 10 points is awarded if the principal applicant's age is between 21 and 49; then points are reduced symmetrically for each year above or below this range. In Australia, in contrast, maximum points are allocated for ages 18 to 29, then reduced for successively older five-year intervals up to age 44. New Zealand's system is generally similar to Australia's in that maximum points are awarded for younger ages (20 to 29), then decrease for successively older age intervals (up to age 55) (Hawthorne 2008, 39-41). Quebec, which has its own point system, awards maximum points for ages 18 to 35, then reduces the allocation by 2 points for each year older than 35 up to age 43, when no points are given. Thus, the Australian, New Zealand, and Quebec systems, by treating age asymmetrically, are offering incentives to demographically desirable younger immigrants (Guillemette and Robson 2006).

In the policy outcome regressions of Appendix Tables A-1 and A-2, the age-points effect is less than half that of the education-points effect (even less if one incorporates the education-completion effects) for principal applicants. In addition, the effect of age on workers' earnings, discussed in Chapter 5, decreases monotonically with age — that is, the fastest gains in workers' earnings occur early in their careers and generally decline in relative terms as they age. Since age is an objective criterion that is easy to measure, making the age points schedule asymmetric might make this dimension of the Canadian point system more effective. As we have already seen, an asymmetric education-points system seems to be operating with quite a strong effect. Indeed, since foreign work experience appears to be so heavily discounted by the Canadian labour market,[13] one might consider reallocating some work-

---

[13] Green and Worswick (2010a) find zero or even negative returns to foreign work experience for recent immigrant arrival cohorts. If we had used these results in this study's calculations, there would actually be no effect to reducing the age at arrival of immigrants.

Table 22: Effects of Changing Weights in the Point System on Immigrants' Skills Outcomes, by Sex

Point System Change	Males	Females
		(change)
Increase in ED weight		
Change in ED *(years)*	0.46	0.46
Change in earnings *(%)*	2.96	3.12
Change in earnings *($)*	1,353.4	1,008.6
Increase in LF weight		
Change in PLF *(% points)*	0.82	0.82
Change in earnings *(%)*	0.97	0.91
Change in earnings *($)*	444.1	293.0
Combined increases		
Change in earnings *(%)*	3.94	4.03
Change in earnings *($)*	1,797.5	1,301.5

ED = Education; AGE = Age; LF = Language Fluency;
PLF = Proportion with host-country language fluency.

Note: The results show only two skill components because the age weight did not change.
Source: Authors' calculations.

experience points to an asymmetric points schedule for age that offers more points to potential immigrants in the more desirable age categories.

Changes in Point System Weights since 1986

As we saw in Table 1 (in Chapter 2), in 1986 Canada's point system began to place greater weights on the skills characteristics of arriving immigrants. What effects, if any, have these changes had on the skills levels and average entry earnings of immigrants arriving under the point system screen since that time? In 1986, maximum points (out of 100) for education were raised from 12 to 25, those for age of arriving immigrants remained unchanged (at 10), and those for language fluency (in either English or French) increased from 15 to 24. The results of our computation of the implications of these changes are shown in Table 22.

It can be seen that these changes to the point system weights are estimated to have raised average education levels of incoming principal applicant immigrants by about half a year and increased their average fluency proportion by close to 1 percentage point. The combined effect of these two skills-level increases thus was to raise the average entry earnings levels by female principal applicants by about 4 percent, or about $1,300, and that of males also by about 4 percent, or about $1,800 per year.

Point System Change	Males		Females
		(change)	
Increase in EXP weight			
Change in EXP *(years)*	0.22		0.22
Change in earnings *(%)*	0.11		0.05
Change in earnings *($)*	48.6		17.3
Combined increases			
Change in earnings *(%)*	4.05		4.08
Change in earnings *($)*	1,846.1		1,318.8

Table 23: Effects of Changing the Point System Weight for Work Experience, by Sex

EXP = Experience
Source: Authors' calculations.

But Table 1 also shows that the maximum points allocated to work experience was also raised over the period from 8 to 21, which should have had an effect on immigrant earnings as well, since more experienced workers are on average more productive in the tasks they can perform in the labour market and hence typically receive higher earnings than less experienced workers. Since years of age and years of work experience in the labour market are tightly linked for a given level of education, we can incorporate the effect of changes in point system weights for experience by assuming that their effect on the average years of work experience of arriving immigrants corresponds to the effect of point system weights for age on the average age of arriving immigrants.[14] The corresponding results are shown in Table 23. Evidently, the increase in experience weights had a negligible effect, the main reason for which is the very high degree of discounting of foreign work experience by the Canadian labour market.

---

14 More formally, $\left.\dfrac{\partial EXP}{\partial PSW_{EXP}}\right|_{PA} = \left.\dfrac{-\partial AGE}{\partial PSW_{AGE}}\right|_{PA}$, where AGE and EXP are years of age and work experience in the labour market. The minus sign reflects that greater age points are intended to favour younger immigrants while greater experience points are intended to attract workers with more experience in working in their given field of endeavour. The above expression is actually a rather conservative assumption since Canada allocates age points symmetrically, with more points given for greater levels of work experience. Obviously, if we could follow immigrants for several years after their arrival, we could better separate out distinct age and work experience effects, especially for women. But for an entry earnings evaluation criterion, there is not much opportunity to do this.

Table 24: Effects of Mid-1990s Revisions to Skilled Immigration Policy on Average Skills and Entry Earnings Levels of Arriving Immigrants, by Sex

Point System Change	Males	Females
	(change)	
Increase in Education weight		
Change in Education *(years)*	0.32	0.32
Change in earnings *(%)*	2.05	2.16
Change in earnings *($)*	937.1	698.3
Increase in Age weight		
Change in Age *(years)*	−0.05	−0.05
Change in earnings *(%)*	−0.02	−0.01
Change in earnings *($)*	−11.2	−4.0
Increase in Language Fluency weight		
Change in PLF *(% points)*	0.55	0.55
Change in earnings *(%)*	0.65	0.60
Change in earnings *($)*	315.4	195.3
Combined increases for Principal Applicants		
Change in earnings *(%)*	2.55	2.76
Change in earnings *($)*	1,241.3	889.6
Change in Economic Class share		
Change in earnings *(%)*	16.6	16.1
Change in earnings *($)*	7,589.3	5,190.6

PLF = Proportion with host-country language fluency.

Source: Authors' calculations.

Mid-1990s Revisions to Skilled Immigration Policy

The mid-1990s saw a major rethink of Canadian immigration policy and its objectives and a greater focus on skilled immigration. The major changes made in this regard (in 1993 and 1996) were to increase the share of immigration coming in under the point system — that is, the Economic Class share — toward a target of 60 percent of all immigrants and to revise point system weights along the lines of a general human capital perspective that put more emphasis on broad, long-run indicators of labour market productivity. From 1986 (when the previous point revision occurred) to 1996, the maximum number of points allocated to education was increased from 12 to 21, those for

Table 25: Canada and Quebec Point System Skills Weights

Skill Characteristic	Canada	Quebec
	(points awarded)	
Education	25	12
Age	10	16
Experience	21	8
Language Fluency	24	22

Source: Authors' calculations.

Table 26: Effects of Adopting Quebec's Point System Skills Weights on the Average Entry Earnings of Arriving Immigrants, by Sex

Point System Change	Males	Females
	(change)	
Change in Education weight		
Change in earnings ($)	–1,353.5	–1,008.6
Change in Age weight		
Changes in earnings ($)	–22.4	–7.4
Change in Experience weight		
Change in earnings ($)	–48.6	–17.3
Change in Language Fluency weight		
Change in earnings ($)	–98.7	–65.1
Combined changes for Principal Applicants		
Change in earnings (%)	–3.33	–3.40
Change in earnings ($)	–1,523.0	–1,098.4

Source: Authors' calculations.

age went up from 10 to 13, and those for language fluency rose from 15 to 21. (Points for work experience went up from 8 to 9 as well, but we disregard this quite modest revision.) Between 1991 and 1997, the Economic Class share of immigration also increased strongly, by about 22 percentage points. We can then ask what effects this package of revisions had on the average skills and entry earnings levels of arriving immigrants. Using the results already obtained, we calculate the estimated effects as shown in Table 24.

As is clearly evident, the increase in the Economic Class share had by far the most dominant effect: a more than 16 percent increase in earnings, compared with the changes in point system weights, which resulted in only a 2.5 to 3 percent increase in earnings. Not only was the Economic Class share increase effect on average entry earnings levels greater by about a factor of six, but it was averaged across *all immigrants*, whereas the effects of the point system weight increases were averaged across only the principal applicants (to which they were applied). As well, among the point system weight changes, that on education had the strongest effect, while that on age was essentially negligible.

Adoption of the Quebec Point System Skill Weights

For some years, Quebec has had its own set of immigration rules and policies (see Boudarbat, Boulet, and Zhu 2007), generally similar to the federal system but operating with rather different point system skills weights than those used by Citizenship and Immigration Canada, as Table 25 shows.[15] Would making the federal point system weights the same as those for the Quebec system for these major skills dimensions increase average entry earnings levels for immigrants to Canada as a whole? The results of our calculations are shown in Table 26.[16]

As can be seen, adopting Quebec's allocation of skills weights actually would reduce average entry earnings levels of landing immigrants as a whole, largely because Quebec's weight on education differs substantially from the federal weight and because the education weight has such a strong effect on average education levels of arriving immigrants. The age and work experience effects are again negligible because of the very weak effect of age weights on the average age outcomes of arriving immigrants. And, while the language fluency weights are quite powerful, the difference in total weights allocated to language proficiency in the two regimes is small (only two points).

---

15 Quebec also allocates up to 6 additional points for education if a diploma or equivalent has been obtained within that province, and 16 points of the language proficiency maximum are allocated for French oral language fluency and 6 points for English oral language fluency. Again, we disregard these differences. The details of Quebec's point system details are available at: http://www.canadavisa.com/quebec-skilled-worker-immigration.html or http://www2.publicationsduquebec.gouv.qc.ca/dynamicSearch/telecharge.php?type=7&file=GPI_3_1_Annexe_2.pdf and http://www.immigration-quebec.gouv.qc.ca/publications/fr/divers/liste-formation.pdf

16 The counterfactual we are considering is the replacement of the maximum weights (for the above skill dimensions) in the Canadian point system by the corresponding weight numbers listed above from the Quebec point system. We do not change the Canadian total points requirement for admission or the total maximum points that could potentially be obtained, both of which also differ between the Canadian and Quebec systems.

Chapter 7

Conclusions and Commentary on Recent Policy Changes

Canadian policy toward skilled immigration is undergoing a dramatic change of direction as immigrants face major challenges to getting ahead in this country. In this volume, we have sought to provide some broad background evidence to improve Canadians' understanding of current concerns and debate on immigration policy. We have examined the effectiveness of Canada's immigration procedures concerning the inflow of skilled immigrants, and highlighted the need to re-examine the operation of federal policy toward these arrivals. To that end, we developed a tool, an evaluative criterion — namely, real annual earnings of workers shortly after their arrival, or average entry earnings — to examine how well immigrants are doing in the Canadian labour market. We then used that criterion to analyze the effect on it of major policy levers of the federal skilled immigration program and of possible changes to those levers. Further, our empirical framework allowed us to put actual dollar figures on the consequences of alternative policy changes. In undertaking this study, we hoped to contribute to moving skilled immigration policy to a more objective, evidence-based approach, as recently recommended in the 2009 auditor general's report.

In Chapter 2, we offered a brief history of the federal skilled immigration system, and reviewed recent changes to the system from an historical perspective. In Chapter 3, we looked at the broad evidence on major changing patterns of immigrants and foreign workers in Canada, and noted the worsening situation for immigrants in the labour market. In Chapter 4, we summarized the findings of a recent study of ours of the effects of major immigration policy levers on the skills characteristics — especially education, age, and language fluency — of arriving immigrants. In Chapter 5, we reviewed the empirical literature on how these newcomers are faring in the labour market and the principal factors that account for their relatively worsening economic situation. Then, in Chapter 6, we developed our empirical framework for evaluating the labour market outcomes of arriving immigrants and presented the results from simulating several policy alternatives and policy changes based on our analysis. In this final chapter, we review our major findings and offer some thoughts on possible reforms to Canadian immigration policy that would benefit not only Canada but those who wish to build their future here.

Review of Major Findings

Our first set of empirical findings refers to estimates of the effects of major policy levers on the average skills levels of arriving immigrants, and is presented in Table 27.

First, increasing the total inflow of immigration generally lowers the average skills levels of arriving immigrants — for example, we estimate that adding 100,000 immigrants a year would reduce the average years of education of incoming immigrants by 0.31. Second, increasing the proportion of immigrants in the Economic Class would raise immigrants' average skills levels — for example, a 10 percentage point rise in that share would raise fluency in either English or French among incoming immigrants by 5.1 percentage points. Third, increasing the weight on specific skills in the federal point system indeed raises average skills levels in those areas among arriving principal applicants — for example, a 10 point increase in the weight on age reduces the average age of principal applicants by 0.17 years — indicating that, basically, the point system works as intended.

In general, the effects of policy levers on education levels and language fluency are relatively strong, while their effects on age are relatively weak. Across all three sets of policy levers, language fluency is most responsive to policy changes in general, education levels are somewhat less responsive, and the age at landing of immigrants is significantly the least responsive. Total inflow and point system weights have a significant effect on immigrants' average education levels, while increasing the Economic Class share has a very strong effect on the average language fluency of arriving immigrants.

The business cycle also has highly significant effects on the skills levels of immigrants arriving in Canada. Generally, higher Canadian unemployment rates reduce those levels and higher US unemployment rates raise them. For example, a 3 percentage point rise in the Canadian rate reduces the average years of education of incoming principal applicants to Canada by 0.29 and increases their average age by 1.54 years, while a similar rise in the US unemployment rate increases the average years of education of

Table 27: Effects of Changes to Major Immigration Policy Levers on the Average Skills Levels of Arriving Immigrants

Policy Change	Years of Education	Age (change)	Percent Fluent
Raise inflow rate by 100,000	−0.31	0.83[a]	−1.1
Raise Economic Class share by 10 points	0.26	−0.27	5.1
Raise point system weight by 10 points (on Principal Applicants)	0.35	−0.17	0.9

a This figure is for Principal Applicants.
Source: Authors' calculations.

principal applicants by 0.59 and reduces their average age by 1.18 years. The mechanism for this effect is likely through the decision on the part of highly skilled applicants waiting in the queue for admission into Canada to decide against coming here during a time of poor labour market conditions, while lower-skilled applicants might not be deterred so easily. We estimate that the recent recession out of which the two countries are climbing raised the average education level of incoming principal applicants by 0.84 years, reduced their average age by 0.81 years, and reduced the average fluency rate by 13 percentage points. These are quite substantial effects.

The human capital model in economics as applied to the immigration literature allowed us to compare differences in skills levels of arriving immigrants and their annual earnings levels shortly thereafter. We present this second set of empirical findings in Table 28.

First, raising the total inflow rate of immigration would reduce the average earnings of arriving female immigrants by about $1,100 per year, while raising the proportion of the Economic Class among total immigrants by 10 percentage points (for a given level of inflow) would increase the entry earnings of arriving male immigrants by about $3,450 per year. Thus, changing the share of the Economic Class is a strong policy lever, and raising this share increases the average earnings of arriving immigrants. Raising the overall level of immigration (holding the immigrant class mix constant) has a moderately strong effect, but works in the direction of reducing the average starting earnings of the new arrivals.[1]

---

1 Keep in mind, though, that these estimates are not general equilibrium results that would allow for rippling feedback effects throughout various sectors of the economy. They are also based on the assumption that policy changes are exogenous and not made in response to the short-run economic outcomes of immigrants.

Table 28: Dollar-Value Effects of Changes to Major Immigration Policy Levers on the Average Entry Earnings of Arriving Immigrants, by Sex

Policy Change	Males	Females
	(change in 2008 dollars)	
Raise inflow rate by 100,000	−1,576	−1,098
Raise Economic Class share by 10 points	3,449	2,357
Raise point system weights by 10 points (for Principal Applicants) for:		
Education	1,042	775
Age	−38	−12
Language Fluency	493	326

Source: Authors' calculations.

Second, increasing the weight on years of education in the point system by 10 points would raise the average entry earnings of female principal applicants by $775 per year, while increasing the weight on language fluency by 10 points would raise the earnings of male principal applicants by $493 per year. Thus, the effect on entry earnings of increasing the weight on points for education is quite strong, the effect of increasing the weight on language fluency is more moderate, and the effect of increasing the weight on age is extremely weak.

Third, education and language fluency are by far the strongest skills channels; the age channel is virtually negligible. The strength of the former two channels reflects both that they are relatively amenable to policy change and that they have strong effects on workers' earnings. Since there is no real return to age, perhaps one could argue that reducing the average age of principal applicants entering under the point system would at least contribute to reducing, if only in a small way, the average rate of aging of the Canadian workforce.

Once again, business cycle effects at the time of landing play an important role. We estimate that the combined effect of increases in the Canadian and US unemployment rates during the recent recession was to reduce average entry earnings of arriving principal applicants by between 8 and 10 percent, or more than $2,700 for women and about $4,550 for men. These reductions are substantial indeed.

Our third set of empirical findings relates to simulations of the effects of several policy changes, both past and possible, and is summarized in Table 29.

Table 29: Dollar-Value Effects of Past and Potential Changes to Major Immigration Policy Levers on the Average Entry Earnings of Arriving Immigrants, by Sex

Policy Change	Males	Females
	(change in 2008 dollars)	
Raise the immigration rate to 1% of population	−1,338	−932
Raise the Economic Class share by 25 percentage points (as between early to mid-1980s and 2000)	8,624	5,898
Changes in point system skill weights since 1986 (for Principal Applicants)	1,846	1,319
Mid-1990s revisions to policy on skilled immigration	7,589	5,191
Adopt Quebec's point system skill weights (for Principal Applicants)	−1,523	−1,098

Source: Authors' calculations.

First, the two changes to policy toward skilled immigration — raising the share of Economic Class immigrants from 35 to 60 percent of the total from the early 1980s to 2000, and a package of several changes introduced in the mid-1990s — improved the average entry earnings of landing immigrants quite substantially. This is not to deny that immigrants' earnings have been falling behind those of other Canadians, but the earnings gap between the two groups would have been even worse in the absence of these policy changes. And, while changes in the point system's weights on skills since 1986 have had a relatively moderately positive effect, raising the total level of immigration to 1 percent of the population or adopting the Quebec point system's skill weights federally would reduce slightly the average earnings levels of incoming immigrants.

The Canadian Experience Program

A further illustration of the approach we developed in this study is provided by an examination of the federal Canadian Experience Class (CEC) program, established in September 2008. This program targets two groups of foreigners that have acquired work experience in the Canadian labour market: temporary foreign workers with at least two years of Canadian work experience in a high-skilled occupation, and post-secondary graduates from a Canadian university or college with one year of Canadian work experience in managerial occupations, professional occupations, or technical occupations and skilled trades. Members of either group can apply for landed immigrant status directly from within Canada, and need not meet the federal skilled worker point system requirements.

The goal of the CEC program can be viewed as attracting immigrants whose skills characteristics can be evaluated more readily by Canadian employers, who can fit more readily into the Canadian labour market because of their Canadian training and familiarity with Canadian employment information networks, and whose fluency on the job in either English or French has already been established in the workplace (see Kato and Sparber 2010; Sweetman and Warman 2010b). The program also side-steps the delays in the processing of applications under the Federal Skilled Worker Program (FSWP). As well, retaining foreign-born graduates with recent Canadian post-secondary education has the additional benefit of attracting younger immigrants.

In terms of the empirical framework of this study, we can represent the potential increases in immigrants' entry earnings by disregarding the discounting by the Canadian labour market of foreign education and work experience.[2] Since these foreign discount factors are quite substantial, the potential increases in entry earnings also could be quite substantial for those affected. As a result, the effect on entry earnings of adding 10 points to the weights on years of education and age at arrival can be recalculated as:

Effect (PSW$_{ED}$ on LYE) = 2.89% (men); 3.61% (women)
Effect (PSW$_{AGE}$ on LYE) = −0.35% (men); −0.35% (women).

The effects of increasing age points are still low because of the symmetric award schedule for such points in the federal point system. Nonetheless, both the education-points and age-points effects are substantially larger — by 27 percent for male immigrants and by 50 percent for females in the case of education — than those reported earlier in Table 16.

Translating these percentage effects into dollar values, the education-points effect increases the entry earnings of male immigrants by $1,319 and

---

2 More formally, we replaced the terms $\frac{\partial LYE}{\partial ED_{FB}}$ and $\frac{\partial LYE}{\partial EXP_{FB}}$, respectively, by $\frac{\partial LYE}{\partial ED_{CB}}$ and $\frac{\partial LYE}{\partial EXP_{CB}}$ in the calculations of point system weight effects for education and age. We applied no such discount for language fluency since we viewed this skill as judged independently of where it was obtained, though it is certainly possible that a foreign accent can have a negative effect.

those of female immigrants by $1,166, while the age-points effect reduces the entry earnings of male immigrants by $158, and those of females by $113. That is, education and work experience — most of which have been acquired abroad — are awarded more highly than would be the case for regular admittees under the skilled worker program. Comparing these figures to those in Table 16, one can see that the potential gains from the Canadian Experience Class program for those who are affected are fairly substantial with respect to the recognition of education credentials. The potential gains through work experience are relatively minor because of the very weak (symmetric) age effects on immigrant earnings.

But who is affected by the advent of the CEC program? The potential gains calculated above refer to immigrants entering under the CEC program who otherwise, we assume, would have been admitted as principal applicants under the FSWP. So the comparisons are between entrants under the CEC and principal applicant entrants under the FSWP. The CEC was implemented in such a way, however, that entrants are counted in the total target of Economic Class immigrants, rather than in addition to it, meaning that any increase in the number of entrants under the CEC will correspondingly reduce the number of entrants under the FSWP. A large number of immigrants are also being admitted outside the FSWP under the Provincial Nominee Program, and many are relatively unskilled, brought in to fill short-run employment gaps. The result of these two recent policy innovations is that the overall share of Economic Class immigrants will decline substantially — by perhaps 10 percentage points, with an associated reduction in the average entry earnings of *all* incoming immigrants of between $2,350 and $3,450 per year, a figure that is much larger and more widespread than is the potential gain to beneficiaries of the CEC program.

Skilled Immigration Policy: A Time to Review

The criterion of immigrant entry earnings and the analytical framework we developed above allow us to contribute some evaluative observations on several specific aspects of Canada's current skilled immigration policy.

First, *emphasize the importance of language fluency in the point system's weights on skills and use an objective approach to assessing applicants' proficiency.* Evidence in Canada and elsewhere strongly supports the importance of language fluency on the job in getting a job commensurate with the immigrant's training and occupational skills and in subsequently advancing in the labour market. It thus makes a lot of sense to put considerable weight in the point system on that skill. Canada, however, has relied on self-declared and informally checked proficiency claims in assessing such points, and is well advised to consider a more formal, objective approach as Australia has followed for more than a decade. We welcome Citizenship and Immigration Canada's statement, in a news release of March 10, 2010, that Canada is indeed moving in the direction where "all applicants are encouraged to submit independent, third-party language test results" — that is, from an objective test. Such an approach would be an improvement, though it might not address fully the difference between general language skills — those likely to be tested — and the specific on-the-job occupational language fluency that is critical to success in the labour market.

Second, and more generally, *maintain current levels of Economic Class immigrants and assess the acceptability of their foreign educational and professional credentials before they arrive*. Australia now operates an apparently more successful point system than Canada (Hawthorne, 2005, 2008). The Economic Class proportion of its total immigration is now running at about 70 percent, compared with 55 to 65 percent in Canada. Since such immigrants invariably perform better in the labour market on average than do other major classes of immigrants (such as the family class or refugees), Canada should consider maintaining the current proportion of Economic Class immigrants — specifically the role of the FSWP — within the immigration system.

Perhaps the key distinguishing feature of the Australian system, however, is that, since 1999, an evaluation is made of a would-be immigrant's professional credentials, language fluency, and so on *before* the applicant lands — that is, an *ex ante* evaluation. In Canada, in contrast, if educational credentials and work experience yield enough points to allow applicants to land, the new arrivals then must undergo the evaluation of their foreign skills and credentials by the Canadian labour market and various provincial and professional bodies — that is, an *ex post* evaluation. Instead, Canada could consider setting up a process of formally assessing foreign degrees, diplomas, and certificates in terms of their Canadian equivalents before the applicant is admitted, while drawing a distinction between educational credentials and the qualifications needed to practise in many professional occupations in Canada.[3] Such a process, however, would require the cooperation of the various regulatory bodies that oversee the professions; moreover, they come under provincial jurisdiction, have their own objectives, and often operate in rather decentralized fashion. Despite these obstacles, the federal and provincial governments recently agreed to put in place, over a three-year period, a process for improving the process of recognizing foreign professional qualifications. We applaud this initiative and urge that it be seen through with persistence and determination.

---

3 The authors wish to thank an anonymous referee for pointing out this important distinction.

Third, *adopt an asymmetric weight scheme for age in the point system.* We found that the effect of the points awarded for age in the federal point system on the earnings outcomes of arriving immigrants is very weak. One way to strengthen this effect would be to move to an asymmetric weight scheme — as both Quebec and Australia currently use — whereby points are reduced for older ages beyond a maximum-points age interval. This asymmetry would attract younger applicants, who, as a number of studies have remarked, do much better in the labour market than those who arrive as adults with foreign education and work experience.

Fourth, *reallocate points away from work experience and toward younger age in the point system.* Foreign work experience is strongly discounted in the Canadian labour market. Part of this revolves around issues with recognizing foreign credentials and professional qualifications, but part also revolves around the ways jobs operate, workplaces are organized, and the technological competence needed in the Canadian context. Thus, since an immigrant's past work experience is not well rewarded, on average, it might make sense to reduce the number of points awarded for work experience in the point system and perhaps reallocate them to younger age instead. In 2004, instead, points allocated for work experience were increased from 9 to 21 and those for age were reduced from 13 to 10. This seems to us a change in the wrong direction. Indeed, the combination of high weight on past work experience and a new emphasis on specified occupations might backfire since the market heavily discounts occupation-specific experience.

Fifth, *do not count immigrants arriving under the Canadian Experience Class program as admissions under the Federal Skilled Worker Program.* The current system has the effect of reducing the Economic Class share of immigration coming in through the point system screen; instead, it would be better to allow the number of immigrants coming in on the basis of their skills (including through the CEC program) to rise.

Sixth, *review the skills of applicants arriving under the Provincial Nominee Program (PNP) and either cap such admissions or allow the cap to vary with the unemployment rate.* The PNP has been criticized for the ad hoc approach provinces take to admissions, the large numbers of relatively low-skilled workers they are admitting — especially in a time of relative economic recession — and for the program's effect of reducing the overall share of skills-assessed immigrants arriving under the FSWP. At the very least, at a time of relatively high unemployment in Canada, it would make sense to undertake a review of the skills profile of applicants arriving under the program and perhaps to put a cap on such admissions, or allow the cap to vary inversely with the overall unemployment rate.

Seventh, *clear up immigration backlogs and processing delays*. If one of the goals of the PNP and other recent policy revisions was to shorten the decision process for skilled worker applicants, then perhaps more resources are needed to reduce the current massive backlog of such applicants. Some processing delays also could be due to the higher processing priority currently being given to programs such as the PNP.[4] Such priorities should be reviewed.

More generally, it would be useful to stand back and consider the broad change in the federal government's perspective on skilled or economic immigration since 2008. The general thrust of the new regulations has been to shift the focus of economic immigration policy from a broad human-capital perspective to a more occupational-gap-filling perspective, from an orientation toward long-run labour market supply to more short-run labour market needs, and from permanent immigration toward greater reliance on temporary foreign workers, even during a period of marked recession. The long-run human-capital model that had dominated Canadian immigration policy since the early nineties — largely in the form of the FSWP and its accompanying point system screen — is now playing a smaller role as immigration policy seeks to become more responsive to the short-run needs of Canadian employers.

This shift in immigration strategy came in response to the worsening of the earnings gap between immigrants and non-immigrants, to lengthy delays in the approval process that have characterized the FSWP, to inadequacies in the current point system, and to the perceived unresponsiveness to labour market shortages and regional labour market needs following a decade and a half of economic growth. Indeed, a major inadequacy of the current federal point system schedule is that it puts a lot of weight on broad white-collar skills and education and little on blue-collar or trade skills and training. Demands for the latter are cyclically sensitive — currently, they are in great demand in the rapidly expanding energy and natural resources sectors in the western provinces.

Clearly, the point system needs to be rethought and restructured to allocate more weight to blue-collar skills to facilitate a more balanced occupational and skills mix among incoming workers. As well, although the maximum number of points for arranged employment was raised from 4 in 1996 to 10 in 2004, arranged employment deserves an even greater weight, with the points perhaps linked to specified trades and other in-demand occupations. The required pass mark in the point system for skilled trades also could be reduced or perhaps varied cyclically so as to reduce admissions when a recession hits.

---

4 We appreciate this observation by an anonymous reviewer.

But how can labour supply and demand considerations, and long-run human capital flexibility, on the one hand, and short-run responsiveness to current labour market needs, be incorporated into Canadian immigration policy? One approach could be to revert to the tap-on/tap-off policies of the 1970s, when intake levels — either in total or by admission category or specific program — were varied with the state of the labour market or the unemployment rate. Current ministerial discretion would certainly allow that strategy, although setting targets would be difficult given the current broad consultative process. But this approach would not address the changing skill mix or specific occupational needs of the Canadian labour market. And despite the recent economic recession, Canada faces a sustained era of relative labour shortages for some time to come as the babyboomers withdraw from the labour market, demand for Canada's natural resources increases in the Pacific Rim countries, and the supply of Canadian-trained skilled trades workers continues to fall short of demand.

At the same time, Canada should resist pressures to bring in large numbers of relatively low-skilled immigrants — even though they might address immediate employment needs. When the economy slows and layoffs occur, these workers likely would be laid off first. Though unemployed, they might prefer to take their chances picking up day-to-day jobs where they can to returning home. The result could be the growth of an underclass of ill-protected and at-risk workers and a potential fiscal burden on the public sector. It could also dampen wage incentives for Canadian-born and permanent immigrant workers to move from regions of relatively higher unemployment and industrial restructuring to regions experiencing economic growth.

In any case, the occupational gap-filling strategy of the 1970s was tried and found wanting. Though perhaps attractive in principle, its implementation problems were considerable. Ottawa developed quite detailed tables of narrowly defined occupations judged to be in demand. It found, however, the tables difficult to keep timely because of the rapid pace of technological and structural change in the economy, the length of time to get usable employment demand survey data and consensus decisions on revised schedules of occupations. In addition, field offices could not keep up with the pace of administrative changes in occupational needs commensurate with changing demand in the economy — applications that satisfied previously designated occupational needs suddenly no longer fit the new sets of occupational needs. There is little reason to expect that such a process could be made to keep pace with evolving employment needs or to be any fairer or more transparent now than in the 1970s.

How, then, should the demand side of the labour market be represented in the selection process for new immigrants? Requiring all applicants under the FSWP to fall into a set number of occupational categories might be worthwhile in the sense that the occupational categories are fairly broad, thus side-stepping some of the past problems with specific occupational targeting. But, as an additional mandatory requirement, it is also quite restrictive, and effectively will reduce the FSWP share of total immigration. A less restrictive and more flexible approach might be to allocate points for broadly defined occupational preferences in the point system itself, perhaps by increasing the number of bonus points for a job offer in hand within those occupations. Additionally, if Ottawa imposes a preference for in-demand occupations that involve the recognition of professional qualifications, then it has a responsibility to assist in the process of facilitating such recognition and dealing with possible gaps in training.

Ottawa is now making heavy use of temporary foreign workers to address short-term skill shortages and temporary tightness in the labour market. Indeed, its use of this program has expanded so rapidly that, since 2007, arrivals under the program — more than half of whom are lower-skilled workers — have exceeded those under the FSWP. In 2010, its numbers exceeded the total number of immigrants arriving in *all* categories. This may be a convenient way to fill employers' immediate needs, but it inhibits the domestic labour market from giving Canadian workers incentives to fill shortages — encouraging employers to become dependent on a continuing supply of foreign workers instead of seeking out domestic alternatives — it opens up temporary workers to possible abuse and exploitation by their sponsoring employers, and it sets the conditions for the creation of a low-wage marginal workforce. Given that Canada's unemployment rate is well above full employment as the economy deals with the effects of a significant recession, it seems reasonable to reduce substantially the numbers of temporary foreign workers, especially the lower skilled, that are being admitted, either by simply putting a cap on such admissions or by linking the level to the unemployment rate.

An insight from the recent literature is the need to recognize and incorporate into the current immigration system the beneficial role of *employer evaluation*. Warman (2007a, 2010) and Sweetman and Warman (2009) find that temporary foreign workers retain the benefits of their foreign human capital and obtain high returns to both their foreign human capital and foreign work experience; indeed, they have higher earnings than immigrant workers with no pre-landing Canadian human capital — although this earnings difference disappears by four years after arrival as the latter group experiences stronger earnings growth. Carter, Pandey, and Townsend (2010) and Pandey and Townsend (2010) also find that immigrants destined for Manitoba under the PNP have earnings similar to, or higher than, those of arrivals under the FSWP in their first year or two years after landing, but that they also experience slower growth in earnings than does the latter group.

What these two sets of studies have in common is the direct evaluation and acceptance of such foreign workers by Canadian employers. We can thus see the benefits of incorporating a *mix* of evaluation approaches into the skilled-worker immigration system. The point system screen for the FSWP addresses broad, long-run economic and social goals of immigration. Employer-based evaluation within the Temporary Foreign Worker Program, the PNP, and, to some degree, the Canadian Experience Class initiative focuses more on the immediate transferability of workers' skills to address short-run labour market needs. Since this imposition of occupational restrictions is an attempt to make policy toward skilled immigration more responsive to such short-run demand, it might make better sense to impose those restrictions on the programs that seek to address those needs, rather than on the FSWP, with its focus on the long-run adaptability of immigrants to the Canadian economy.

A selection system for skilled labour reasonably should have several components and be multi-tracked in order to satisfy a range of needs. One route, the standard Federal Skilled Worker Program, seeks to provide an effective way to choose highly skilled individuals and those with good potential to contribute to the Canadian labour market and who may not have pre-arranged employment. The Canadian Experience Class provides an opportunity for those who have already demonstrated adaptability to the Canadian environment and eases their application process. Such a system also could allow employers to nominate workers with some required level of skills because of their potential to find immediate and successful labour market matches, and temporary foreign workers to fill short-term labour shortages in times of economic growth and tightening labour markets. These should be viewed as complements to the FSWP, not as substitutes for it. Current problems with the FSWP should be addressed by modifying the program, not by scaling it back. Flexibility and nimbleness of adjustment should be important in the selection process for skilled immigrants, but so also should be transparency and timeliness of response and a consideration of long-run gains.

Canada's immigration system will always have to deal with short-term pressures, but immigration-related decisions also have longer-run implications. The current system has not undergone a major review since the mid-1990s, and an examination now seems due — one that looks at the longer-run role and objectives of immigration in Canada's future and how best to meet these objectives.

Appendix A:

Table A-1: Regression Results for Years of Education

	All Immigration	Economic Principal Applicants
Economic Class	2.639**	n.a.
(vs Family Class)	(.0052)	
Time trend	0.1984**	0.1800**
	(.0014)	(.0024)
Total inflow (in '000s)	−0.00310**	−0.00211**
	(.000084)	(.00015)
Economic share of inflow	−0.00051	0.01338**
(out of 100)	(.00057)	(.00099)
Education points	0.01397**	0.03534**
(out of 100)	(.00081)	(.00143)
Indicator for 1993 or later	−0.2001**	0.4150**
	(.0102)	(.0197)
Canadian unemployment rate	−0.0921**	−0.0967**
	(.0036)	(.0059)
US unemployment rate	0.2045**	0.1958**
	(.0047)	(.0082)
R^2	0.1760	0.1602
P-value for F test	<0.0001	<0.0001
RMSE	3.642	3.378
Sample size	2,683,524	753,137

Notes: Standard errors are presented in parentheses. ** and * denote significant at 1 percent and 5 percent levels, respectively. The regressions also include controls for other admission classes (in the AI regression), region of residence, and source region.
Source: Parameter estimates from Beach, Green, and Worswick (2008).

Table A-2: Regression Results for Age at Immigration

	All Immigration	Economic Principal Applicants
Economic Class	−6.501**	n.a.
(vs Family Class)	(.018)	
Time trend	−0.0815**	0.0487**
	(.0044)	(.0055)
Total inflow (in '000s)	−0.00290**	0.00826**
	(.00030)	(.00038)
Economic share of inflow	0.0377**	−0.0244**
(out of 100)	(.0019)	(.0023)
Age points	0.03720**	−0.01707**
(out of 100)	(.0029)	(.0037)
Canadian unemployment rate	0.1690**	0.5144**
	(.0119)	(.0143)
US unemployment rate	0.0132**	−0.3926**
	(.0174)	(.0220)
R^2	0.0728	0.0315
P-value for F test	<0.0001	<0.0001
RMSE	13.126	8.520
Sample size	2,789,599	757,436

Notes: Standard errors are presented in parentheses. ** and * denote significant at 1 percent and 5 percent levels, respectively. The regressions also include controls for other admission classes (in the AI regression), region of residence, and source region.
Source: Parameter estimates from Beach, Green, and Worswick (2008).

Table A-3: Regression Results for English- or French-Language Fluency

	All Immigration	Economic Principal Applicants
Economic Class	0.2605**	n.a.
(vs Family Class)	(.00060)	
Time trend	0.00309**	−0.00547**
	(.00016)	(.00025)
Total inflow (in '000s)	−0.00011**	0.000089**
	(.00000)	(.00001)
Economic share of inflow	0.00246**	0.00362**
(out of 100)	(.000065)	(.00011)
Language points	0.00168**	0.00091**
(out of 100)	(.00012)	(.00020)
Canadian unemployment rate	0.02470**	0.04281**
	(.00037)	(.00055)
US unemployment rate	−0.00275**	−0.04317**
	(.00049)	(.00076)
R^2	0.1896	0.0935
P-value for F test	<0.0001	<0.0001
RMSE	0.4339	0.3581
Sample size	2,789,626	757,438

Notes: Standard errors are presented in parentheses. ** and * denote significant at 1 percent and 5 percent levels, respectively. The regressions also include controls for other admission classes (in the AI regression), region of residence, and source region.
Source: Parameter estimates from Beach, Green, and Worswick (2008).

Table A-4: Basic Earnings Regressions for Immigrant and Canadian-Born Men: Immigrant Earnings Adjustment by Arrival Cohort (dependent variable is the log of annual earnings)

	Arrival Cohort Shifts	Arrival Cohort-YSL Interactions
Immigrant status	−.22 (.019)*	−.12 (.025)*
Arrival cohort dummies:		
1983–86 cohort	−.18 (.0087)*	−.22 (.020)*
1987–89 cohort	−.16 (.012)*	−.21(.028)*
1990–92 cohort	−.35 (0.16)*	−.54 (.033)*
1993–96 cohort	−.41 (0.23)*	−.64 (.044)*
Years since landing:		
YSL	.065 (.0040)*	.035 (.0058)*
YSL^2	−.0039 (.00024)*	−.0014 (.00031)*
Arrival cohort-YSL interactions:		
1983–86 cohort	/	.0068 (.0026)*
1987–89 cohort	/	.0089 (.0044)*
1990–92 cohort	/	.048 (.0068)*
1993–96 cohort	/	.10 (.016)*
Education level:		
High school	−.23 (.0065)*	−.23 (.0064)*
University	.26 (.0082)*	.26 (.0078)*
Work experience:		
EXP	.034 (.0015)*	.034 (.0015)*
EXP^2	−.00057 (.000032)*	−.00057 (.000031)*
NOBS	2442	2442
R^2	.85	.86

Notes: The regressions also include an intercept and individual year dummies. Figures in parentheses are White standard errors. * indicates statistically significantly different from zero at the 5 percent level of significance. The default education level is post-secondary. Immigrant and Canadian-born workers are pooled in each of the two regressions.
Source: Green and Worswick (2002), table 1.

Table A-5: Earnings Regressions for Immigrant and Canadian-Born Men: Immigrant Earnings Adjustment by Education and Age at Landing (dependent variable is the log of annual earnings)

	High School				Post-secondary				University			
	Age 25–29	Age 30–34	Age 35–39	Age 40–44	Age 25–29	Age 30–34	Age 35–39	Age 40–44	Age 25–29	Age 30–34	Age 35–39	Age 40–44
Immigrant status	−.21* (.047)	−.18* (.036)	−.056 (.058)	−.010 (.061)	.095* (.049)	.28* (.060)	.31* (.064)	.27* (.068)	−.027 (.084)	.22* (.082)	.40* (.084)	.49* (.091)
Arrival cohort dummies:												
1983–86 cohort	−.062 (.043)	−.033 (.043)	.015 (.059)	−.0025 (.063)	−.40* (.048)	−.45* (.058)	−.35* (.068)	−.28* (.071)	−.099 (.073)	−.062 (.073)	−.064 (.080)	.077 (.089)
1987–89 cohort	−.029 (.054)	.16* (.047)	−.052 (.080)	−.087 (.065)	−.092 (.065)	−.29* (.070)	−.20* (.068)	−.26* (.071)	−.13 (.097)	−.19* (.093)	−.35* (.097)	−.40* (.11)
1990–92 cohort	−.14* (.062)	−.13* (.054)	−.23* (.069)	−.29* (.080)	−.35* (.059)	−.57* (.070)	−.66* (.087)	−.43* (.097)	−.32* (.099)	−.37* (.097)	−.53* (.11)	−.59* (.11)
1993–96 cohort	−.23* (0.70)	−.29* (.064)	−.58* (.085)	−.45* (0.97)	−.31* (.081)	−.51* (.090)	−.57* (.097)	−.47* (.097)	−.24* (.095)	−.58* (.11)	−.75* (.090)	−.82* (.12)
Years since landing:												
YSL	.031 (.010)	.037 (.0099)	.013 (.016)	−.0017 (.017)	−.018 (.011)	−.035 (.014)	−.042 (.014)	−.037 (.015)	.0051 (.019)	−.028 (.018)	−.047 (.019)	−.043 (.017)
YSL²	−.0019 (.00055)	−.0021 (.00061)	−.0012 (.00086)	−.00076 (.00098)	.0012 (.00063)	.0015 (.00073)	.0016 (.00075)	.00086 (.00082)	−.00022 (.00093)	.00084 (.00093)	.0014 (.00099)	−.00012 (.0011)
Arrival cohort-YSL interactions:												
1983–86 cohort	.0078 (.0051)	−.0017 (.0053)	−.0093 (.0075)	−.0026 (.0094)	.012* (.006)	.018* (.007)	.011 (.0083)	.0086 (.0091)	.00014 (.0086)	−.0038 (.0086)	−.0046 (.0092)	−.0026 (.011)
1987–89 cohort	−.0019 (.0082)	−.0027 (.0076)	.0044 (.013)	.011 (.011)	.0021 (.0099)	.010 (.010)	.0078 (.0097)	.015 (.011)	.015 (.014)	.018 (.014)	.027 (.014)	.013 (.015)
1990–92 cohort	.0025 (.013)	−.0016 (.013)	.0097 (.015)	.027 (.018)	.034* (.012)	.059* (.013)	.079* (.017)	.038 (.021)	.024 (.017)	.029 (.017)	.031 (.019)	.031 (.019)
1993–96 cohort	.028 (.032)	−.0020 (.031)	.100* (.037)	.021 (.048)	.0013 (.024)	.052 (.027)	.069* (.030)	.0012 (.027)	.025 (.031)	.13* (.035)	.14* (.026)	.090* (.041)

Notes: The regressions also include an intercept and a detrended unemployment rate. Figures in parentheses are White standard errors. *indicates statistically significantly different from zero at the 5 percent level of significance. Immigrant and Canadian-born workers are pooled in each of the twelve regressions.
Source: Green and Worswick (2002), table 3.

Table A-6: Earnings Regressions for Economic Immigrant and Canadian-Born Men: Immigrant Earnings Adjustment by Education and Age at Landing (dependent variable is the log of annual earnings)

	High School				Post-secondary				University			
	Age 25–29	Age 30–34	Age 35–39	Age 40–44	Age 25–29	Age 30–34	Age 35–39	Age 40–44	Age 25–29	Age 30–34	Age 35–39	Age 40–44
Immigrant status	-.16*	.032	.022	.14*	.17*	.26*	.29*	.27*	.093	.23*	.40*	.56*
	(.041)	(.029)	(.047)	(.040)	(.036)	(.038)	(.036)	(.043)	(.051)	(.051)	(.053)	(.060)
Arrival cohort dummies:												
1983–86 cohort	-.048	-.13*	-.15*	-.15*	-.32*	-.34*	-.29*	-.31*	-.052	.023	-.021	-.047
	(.028)	(.025)	(.029)	(.031)	(.026)	(.027)	(.028)	(.030)	(.033)	(.031)	(.033)	(.043)
1987–89 cohort	.010	.010	-.037	-.15*	-.069*	-.18*	-.17*	-.18*	-.066	-.082*	-.20*	-.32*
	(.030)	(.027)	(.035)	(.032)	(.025)	(.027)	(.024)	(.028)	(.039)	(.038)	(.037)	(.050)
1990–92 cohort	-.027	-.17*	-.21*	-.29*	-.17*	-.30*	-.34*	-.30*	-.20*	-.24*	-.37*	-.51*
	(.040)	(.035)	(.039)	(.044)	(.029)	(.032)	(.034)	(.035)	(.049)	(.045)	(.046)	(.053)
1993–96 cohort	.010	-.35*	-.42*	-.53*	-.22*	-.33*	-.38*	-.45*	-.15*	-.28*	-.41*	-.66*
	(.055)	(.049)	(.056)	(.055)	(.043)	(.049)	(.047)	(.044)	(.055)	(.049)	(.061)	(.068)
Years since landing:												
YSL	.030	.0061	.015	.0067	-.020*	-.014	-.014	-.013	.010	-.0082	-.032*	-.047*
(.0094)	(.0075)	(.012)	(.011)	(.0089)	(.0088)	(.0088)	(.0097)	(.012)	(.012)	(.012)	(.014)	
YSL2	-.0016*	-.00057	-.0018*	-.0015*	.0016*	.00056	.000015	-.00069	-.00060	-.00027	.00050	.00022
	(.00055)	(.00048)	(.00075)	(.00069)	(.00052)	(.00052)	(.00052)	(.00058)	(.00069)	(.00073)	(.00074)	(.00084)

Notes: The regressions also include an intercept and a detrended unemployment rate. Figures in parentheses are White standard errors. * indicates statistically significantly different from zero at the 5 percent level of significance. Immigrant and Canadian-born workers are pooled in each of the twelve regressions.
Source: Green and Worswick (2002), table 5.

Appendix B:
Detailed Calculations for Chapter 4

In this appendix, we provide more detail on how we calculated the policy lever effects on immigrant skills levels, discussed in Chapter 4. The calculations are based on the regression results provided in Appendix Tables A-1 to A-3.

Effects on Years of Education

The effect of an increase by 1,000 immigrants per year on the average number of years of education of arriving immigrants is given by the partial derivative of level of immigration (LOM) on years of education (ED) in column 1 of Table A-1:

$$\left.\frac{\partial ED}{\partial LOM}\right|_{AI} = -.00310.$$

So an increase in immigration levels by 100,000 arrivals per year is 100 times this amount, or a reduction of -.31 of a year of education.*

The effect of an increase by 1 percentage point in the Economic Class share (ECS) of a given level of immigration on the years of education of arriving immigrants is given by the combined coefficients in column 1 of Table A-1:

$$\left.\frac{\partial ED}{\partial ECS}\right|_{AI} = 2.639\times(.01)-.00051 = .02588$$

where the Economic Class shift coefficient is rescaled into percentage point terms. So an increase in ECS by 10 percentage points implies an increase in average years of education of arriving immigrants of ten times this amount, or .26 of a year.

If the increase of 100,000 immigrants per year is all in the Economic Class, both LOM and ECS change together. To calculate the ECS component of this combined effect, suppose the number of Economic Class arrivals goes up

---

* It should be noted that, in multiplying up a derivative or marginal effect in order to calculate a discrete increment, we are using a convenient approximation rather than an exact calculation.

from its recent level of about 60 percent of the total number of immigrants (that is .60 × 250,000, or 150,000) to a new level of 250,000, while total immigration rises from 250,000 to 350,000 per year. The Economic Class share then rises from .60 to 250/350 = .714, or by 11.4 percentage points. The combined effect on years of education is given by

$$100 \times \frac{\partial ED}{\partial LOM}\bigg|_{AI} + 11.4 \times \frac{\partial ED}{\partial ECS}\bigg|_{AI} = -.310 + .295 = -.015.$$

Note, incidentally, that the 100,000 increase in Economic Class immigrants is not the same as a 100,000 increase in principal applicants. On average, there are 2.3 Economic Class arrivals — such as an accompanying spouse and dependent children — for each principal applicant (Beach, Green, and Worswick 2008, 371). So a 100,000 increase in Economic Class immigrants would correspond to approximately 43,500 additional principal applicants per year.

The effect of increasing the weight on years of education in the point system schedule by 1 percentage point is given by the corresponding coefficient in column 2 of Table A-1:

$$\frac{\partial ED}{\partial PSW_{ED}}\bigg|_{PA} = .03534.$$

So raising the education weight by 10 percentage points increases the average level of education of arriving principal applicants by ten times this amount, or .35 of a year. But the regression results also show that awarding points for having a university degree raises the incoming education level by .415 of a year. So the combined effect of both these weight changes is to raise the average level of education of incoming principal applicants by .77 of a year.

Unemployment rates also have highly statistically significant effects on the average education level of arriving immigrants. From the second column of Table A-1, one can see that

$$\frac{\partial ED}{\partial UR_C}\bigg|_{PA} = -.0967.$$

for a 1 percentage point rise in the Canadian unemployment rate, and

$$\left.\frac{\partial ED}{\partial UR_{US}}\right|_{PA} = .1958.$$

for a 1 point increase in the US unemployment rate. Thus, the effects of a 3 point rise in each are given by three times these amounts, or −.29 and .59 of a year, respectively.

Effects on Age at Landing

The policy lever effects on the average age (AGE) of landing immigrants are taken from the regression coefficients in Table A-2.

The effect on average age of increasing total immigration by 1,000 per year is given by the coefficient

$$\left.\frac{\partial AGE}{\partial LOM}\right|_{PA} = .00826.$$

So increasing the total inflow by 100,000 immigrants per year raises the average age of principal applicants by 100 times this amount, or .83 of a year.

The effect of a 1 percentage point increase in the Economic Class share is given by the coefficients

$$\left.\frac{\partial AGE}{\partial ECS}\right|_{AI} = -6.501\times(.01)+.0377 = -.0273.$$

So a 10 point increase in the Economic Class share is estimated to reduce the average age at arrival by .27 of a year.

If the 100,000 increase in number of immigrants occurs just in the Economic Class, the combined effect of the increase in LOM and rise in ECS is given by

$$100\times\left.\frac{\partial PLF}{\partial LOM}\right|_{AI} +11.4\times\left.\frac{\partial PLF}{\partial ECS}\right|_{AI} = -.011+.05774 = -.04674.$$

The effect of increasing the weight on an applicant's age in the point system schedule by 1 percentage point is

$$\left.\frac{\partial AGE}{\partial PSW_{AGE}}\right|_{PA} = -.01707.$$

So increasing this weight by 10 points implies a reduction in average age by .17 of a year.

Unemployment rates have a highly statistically significant effect on average age at arrival, where

$$\left.\frac{\partial AGE}{\partial UR_C}\right|_{PA} = .5144 \quad \text{and} \quad \left.\frac{\partial AGE}{\partial UR_{US}}\right|_{PA} = -.3926$$

for the Canadian and US unemployment rates, respectively. So a 3 percentage point rise in the Canadian rate increases the average age at arrival by 1.54 years, while a similar rise in the US rate reduces the average age at arrival by −1.18 years .

Effects on Language Fluency

The policy lever effects on the proportion of arriving immigrants claiming to be fluent in either English or French are taken from the regression coefficient results in Table A-3.

The effect of increase the number of immigrants by 1,000 per year on the proportion with host-country language fluency (PLF) is given by the coefficient

$$\left.\frac{\partial PLF}{\partial LOM}\right|_{AI} = -.00011.$$

So a 100,000 increase in total annual inflow reduces the proportion that is fluent in English or French by .011 — a small but nonetheless statistically significant amount.

The effect on language fluency of a 1 percentage point increase in the Economic Class share is reported as

$$\left.\frac{\partial PLF}{\partial ECS}\right|_{AI} = .2605 \times (.01) + .00246 = .005065.$$

So a 10 point increase in the Economic Class share raises average fluency percentage by 5.1 percentage points.

Again, an increase of 100,000 Economic Class immigrants per year is given by the combined effect

$$100 \times \frac{\partial PLF}{\partial LOM}\bigg|_{AI} + 11.4 \times \frac{\partial PLF}{\partial ECS}\bigg|_{AI} = -.011 + .05774 = .04674,$$

or an increase in the average fluency rate of 4.7 percentage points.

The effect of increasing the point system weight on fluency in either English or French by 1 percentage point is estimated as

$$\frac{\partial PLF}{\partial PSW_{LF}}\bigg|_{AI} = .00091.$$

So increasing this weight by 10 points implies an increase in the average fluency rate of .91 of a percentage point.

The effects of unemployment rates increasing by 1 percentage point are given by the coefficients

$$\frac{\partial PLF}{\partial UR_C}\bigg|_{PA} = .04281 \quad \text{and} \quad \frac{\partial PLF}{\partial UR_{US}}\bigg|_{PA} = -.04317.$$

Calculations for Table 13

The percentage effects in Table 13 were obtained by making use of the results calculated above and expressing these effects as a percentage of the (approximate) sample means:

Mean (ED) = 11 years   for all immigrants
Mean (AGE) = 29 years   for all immigrants
Mean (PLF) = .56   for all immigrants
Mean (ED) = 13 years   for principal applicants
Mean (AGE) = 26 years   for principal applicants
Mean (PLF) = .75   for principal applicants.

So, for example, the effect on ED of an increase of 100,000 immigrants a year is a reduction in the average level of education of incoming immigrants of .310 of a year. Divide this by the average education level of 11 years over the sample period covered by the analysis (1980–2001), and the percentage effect is -.310/11 = -.0282, or a reduction of 2.8 percent. Other entries in the table are calculated analogously.

Calculations for Table 14

The approach to measuring the relative strength of alternative policy levers on the skills outcomes of immigrants is to ask how large a policy lever change would need to be to generate a given specified change in average skills outcomes. The required change in the average level of education is half a year. The required change in the average age at time of arrival is also half a year. And the required change in the proportion of incoming immigrants fluent in either English or French is 0.5 of a percentage point.

Now, the results in Table A-1 indicate that an increase of 1,000 immigrants per year in the level of immigration (LOM) reduces the average education level of incoming immigrants by .00310 of a year. That is,

$$\frac{\partial ED}{\partial LOM}\bigg|_{AI} = -.00310.$$

So Z is the multiple of this such that the outcome of a decrease in average education levels is .5:

$$Z \times \frac{\partial ED}{\partial LOM}\bigg|_{AI} = -.5,$$

or Z × (−.00310) = −.5, or Z = (.5)/(.00310) = 161.3. Each of the other entries in Table 14 is calculated analogously.

Calculations for Table 15

Entries in the first panel of Table 15 are calculated the same way as in Table 13. In the third panel, calculations make use of the following data: (i) between January 2008 and August 2009, the Canadian unemployment rate rose from 6.0 percent to 8.7 percent, or by 2.7 percentage points; and (ii) between 2007 and the third quarter of 2009, the US unemployment rate went up from

4.6 percent to 10.2 percent, or by 5.6 percentage points (Statistics Canada 2010, 18, 71). If

$$\frac{\partial ED}{\partial UR_C}\bigg|_{PA} = -.0967 \quad \text{and} \quad \frac{\partial ED}{\partial UR_{US}}\bigg|_{PA} = .1958,$$

then the combined effect of a 2.7 point rise in the Canadian unemployment rate and a 5.6 point rise in the US rate is given by

$$2.7 \times \left[\frac{\partial ED}{\partial UR_C}\right] + 5.6 \times \left[\frac{\partial ED}{\partial UR_{US}}\right] = .8354,$$

which is the first entry in this panel. The remaining two entries are calculated similarly. The entries in the second panel of the table are calculated by dividing each of the panel's three entries by their corresponding sample mean outcome values, as done in Table 13.

Appendix C:
Detailed Calculations for Chapter 6, Effects of Immigrants' Skills Levels on Their Earnings

This appendix makes use of published results in the literature to calculate estimates of the effects of immigrants' skills levels on their earnings, as presented in Chapter 6. We undertake the analysis in terms of partial derivatives of estimated regression functions, where the dependent or outcome variable is the logarithm of workers' earnings (LYE). In the text discussion of Chapter 6, we use the term "Effect (x on y)" — this is shorthand for a partial derivative. So, for example, the effect of a marginal change in the level of immigration (LOM) on the average years of education of arriving immigrants is given by

$$\text{Effect (LOM on ED)} = \left.\frac{\partial ED}{\partial LOM}\right|_{AI}.$$

Effect of Education on Earnings

The first effect we have to quantify is that of education on immigrants' earnings or, in the terminology of Chapter 5, the return to immigrants' educational attainment (in terms of years of education):

$$\left.\frac{\partial LYE}{\partial ED}\right|_{FB}.$$

This corresponds to the effect of different levels of education on workers' earnings. A relevant set of earnings equations for immigrants (or foreign-born, FB) and Canadian-born (CB) workers is found in Green and Worswick (2002, table 1) summarized here in Appendix Table A-4. The education effects on earnings in Table A-4, however, are for men, and are expressed in terms of the dummy variable coefficients for workers with high school education (−.23) and for university educated workers (+.26). These are (proportional) differentials relative to the default category of college education. So the earnings difference between the top and bottom education categories is .49. If we assume that the bottom education group has, on average, 11 years of education, the college educated have 14 years, and the university educated have 17 years, then the .49 earnings differential points can be spread over $17 - 11 = 6$ years. Thus, for Canadian-born male workers,

$$\left.\frac{\partial LYE}{\partial ED}\right|_{CB} = \frac{.49}{6} = .0817,$$

where CB indicates Canadian-born. This calculation does not incorporate distinct sheepskin effects associated with the final year that completes a program, but it is nonetheless a reasonable value from the empirical literature. Aydemir and Skuterud (2005) provide separate estimates of the returns to years of education for males and females based on pooled data from several Canadian censuses, including that of 2001. Since their estimate for males is very close to the our result, we adopt their estimate of the return to years of education for (Canadian-born) females of .1022 (Aydemir and Skuterud 2005, table 1).

But, as the literature review in Chapter 5 notes, Canadian employers generally discount the returns to foreign education. Again, Aydemir and Skuterud (2005, table 1) provide estimates of the discount to years of foreign education of 21.1 percent for males and 33.5 percent for females. Thus, the returns to years of education for immigrant males can be estimated as .0817 $[1 - .211]$ = .0645, and that for immigrant females as .1022 $[1 - .335]$ = .0680. Skuterud and Su (2009) obtain somewhat lower discount rates for foreign education, while Bonikowska, Green, and Riddell (2008) report considerably higher discount rates. Thus, we use the estimates

$$\left.\frac{\partial LYE}{\partial ED}\right|_{FB} = .0645 \text{ for males and } \left.\frac{\partial LYE}{\partial ED}\right|_{FB} = .0680 \text{ for females.}$$

Effect of Work Experience on Earnings

For a given level of education, differences in age correspond to differences in years of work experience. The experience effect, then, corresponds to the effect of different amounts of work experience on workers' earnings. Again, a relevant set of earnings equations capturing this effect is found in Green and Worswick (2002, table 1), provided here in Appendix Table A-4. The age effect in that table corresponds to the experience effect

$$\left.\frac{\partial LYE}{\partial EXP}\right|_{CB} = .034 - .00114EXP,$$

which is the slope or first derivative of the quadratic work experience terms in column 2 of Table A-4. The return to work experience differs with age — younger workers generally earn a higher return because of their longer payback period and lower early earnings and older workers earn a lower rate of return. If we assume that workers started school at age 6, that the average age of arriving immigrants is 30, and the average years of education of arriving immigrants is 12 — see Figures 1 and 2 — then average years of work experience for male immigrants at time of landing is about 12. Plugging this into the above expression yields an average rate of return of .0203, or 2.0 percent higher earnings. Ferrer and Riddell (2008, table 3), also using data from multiple Canadian censuses, including that of 2001, provide separate estimates of the return to work experience for males and females, and theirs for males is virtually identical to our result. So we adopt their corresponding estimate of the return to work experience for females:

$$\left.\frac{\partial LYE}{\partial EXP}\right|_{CB} = .034 - .00112EXP.$$

Evaluating this at 12 years of experience yields a return of .0206.

But again, these rates of return to work experience are essentially relevant to Canadian-born workers, with foreign work experience severely discounted in the Canadian labour market. Ferrer and Riddell (2008, table 3) estimate the foreign-experience discount rates as 76.4 percent for males and 88.3 percent for females. Thus, we can estimate the returns to work experience for immigrant males as .0203 [1 − .764] = .00479, and those for immigrant females as .0206 [1 − .883] = .00241.[*] The estimates are thus

$$\left.\frac{\partial LYE}{\partial EXP}\right|_{FB} = .00479 \text{ for males and } \left.\frac{\partial LYE}{\partial EXP}\right|_{FB} = .00241 \text{ for females.}$$

---

[*] Similar very high discount rates for foreign work experience are found in Skuterud and Su (2009) and in Bonikowska, Green, and Riddell (2008).

We may note that Green and Worswick (2002) find that the returns to foreign work experience were still positive and statistically significant for immigrants landing in the early 1980s, but effectively became zero or even negative in the 1990s and remain so for more recent arrivals. Had we made use of the more recent cohorts' returns to foreign work experience, the estimated effects would have been weaker still.

Effect of Language Fluency on Earnings

Finally, we calculate the effect of the language fluency of arriving immigrants on their entry earnings levels. To get estimates of this from evidence available in the research literature, note that

$$\left.\frac{\partial LYE}{\partial PLF}\right|_{FB} = \left.\frac{\partial LYE}{\partial LIT}\right|_{FB} \times \left.\frac{dLIT}{dPLF}\right|_{FB} = \left.\frac{\partial LYE}{\partial LIT}\right|_{FB} \times \left.\frac{dPLF}{dLIT}\right|_{FB}^{-1},$$

where LIT represents a language fluency test score and PLF is the proportion of arriving immigrants fluent in either English or French. So the first component represents the effect of language fluency test scores on immigrant workers' earnings levels, and the second component represents a conversion rate between immigrants' language fluency test scores and the proportion of arriving immigrants identified as fluent in either English or French.[*] There are considerable challenges in the assessment of the effect of language fluency on workers' earnings. Perhaps the best source of language fluency test results for Canada comes from Statistics Canada's 2003 International Adult Literacy and Skills Survey (IALSS). The survey also includes standard demographic and labour market information, including earnings of both immigrants and Canadian-born workers. This allows us to estimate directly the effects of standardized measures of prose and document literacy on earnings. More details on these measures can be found in Bonikowska, Green, and Riddell (2008, sect. 3). Note, however, that these measures capture fluency in general use rather than on-the-job or workplace fluency, which would be preferable (see Weiner 2008).

---

[*] For convenience, we represent the latter as a total, rather than as a partial effect potentially dependent on yet other factors.

Estimates of the effects of literacy test scores for immigrants and Canadian-born workers (controlling for workers' education and work experience) are also found in Bonikowska, Green, and Riddell (2008, tables 5.4, 5.5). For male immigrants with no Canadian education,

$$\left. \frac{\partial LYE}{\partial LIT} \right|_{FB} = .00408$$

the corresponding figure for female immigrants is .00373. We are not aware of estimates of the marginal rate conversion factor in the second component, but if we assume the marginal rate is approximately equal to the average rate at which higher average fluency test scores of arriving immigrants are associated with higher average fluency rates, we can approximate the conversion factor by

$$\left. \frac{AvgPLF}{AvgLIT} \right|_{FB}^{-1}.$$

By taking an average of prose and document literacy test scores from Bonikowska, Green, and Riddell (2008, tables 3.3, 3.4), we obtain Avg LIT = 245.0 for males and 246.5 for females. If we take the corresponding scores of Canadian-born workers as the norm for full language fluency, we can calculate, again for prose and document literary tests, that Avg PLF = .842 for male and .830 for female immigrants. Studies by Ferrer, Green and Riddell (2006) and by Alboim, Finnie and Meng (2005) find similar valued literacy scores. So, for males, .842/245 = .003437. That is, a 10 point higher average fluency test score corresponds to a rise in the average fluency rate of .0344 — from, say, .842 to .876. in other words, PLF, the proportion that is fluent, goes up proportionally with higher immigrant average literacy test scores. The corresponding figure for females is .003367. The term $\frac{\partial LYE}{\partial PLF}$ then is calculated as

$$\left. \frac{\partial LYE}{\partial PLF} \right|_{FB} = \left. \frac{\partial LYE}{\partial LIT} \right|_{FB} \times \left. \frac{AvgPLF}{AvgLIT} \right|_{FB}^{-1}.$$

$$= (.00408) \times (.003437)^{-1}$$
$$= 1.1871$$

for immigrant males and 1.1078 for females. While these figures are for the entire stock of Canadian immigrants in 2003 who had received no Canadian education, we perhaps can reasonably assume that a similar conversion factor ratio between average PLF and average LIT would hold for arriving immigrants as well.

Appendix D:
Detailed Calculations for Chapter 6, Policy Lever Effects on Immigrants' Earnings

In this appendix, we provide details on the calculations of the policy lever effects on immigrant earnings discussed in Chapter 6. The appendix essentially links the calculations presented in Appendix B, on the policy lever effects on immigrants' skills levels, and Appendix C, on the effects of skills levels on immigrants' earnings. Once again, the term in the text "Effect (x on y)" is shorthand for the partial derivative $\frac{\partial y}{\partial x}$ that we use in this appendix. The calculated effects are presented in the same order as in Chapter 6.

Level of Immigration (LOM)

The effect operates through three skills-related channels: on the average education level of arriving immigrants, on their average age, and on the proportion fluent in either English or French. We consider each of these in turn.

The effect operating through years of education, ED, of arriving immigrants is given by

$$\left.\frac{\partial LYE}{\partial LOM}\right|_{ED} = \left.\frac{\partial ED}{\partial LOM}\right|_{AI} \times \left.\frac{\partial LYE}{\partial ED}\right|_{FB} , \tag{1}$$

where LYE is the (log of) workers' earnings, LOM is the level of immigration inflow, and ED is the average education level (in terms of number of years of education) of arriving immigrants. The effect of changing immigration levels on average earnings of arriving immigrants operating through the channel of their average education level can be seen to depend on two terms: how immigration levels affect the average education level (the first term above), and how the level of education affects immigrants' expected earnings (the second term). The first term is given by estimation results for "all immigrants" (AI) in the first column of Appendix Table A-1, as detailed in Appendix B:

$$\left.\frac{\partial ED}{\partial LOM}\right|_{AI} = -.00310.$$

The second term is obtained from the research literature, as detailed in Appendix C:

$$\left.\frac{\partial LYE}{\partial ED}\right|_{FB} = .0645 \text{ for males and } \left.\frac{\partial LYE}{\partial ED}\right|_{FB} = .0680 \text{ for females.}$$

Consequently combining these two effects in equation (1), the estimated effect of increasing the total level of immigration by, say, 100,000 immigrants per year is given by:

$$\left.\frac{\partial LYE}{\partial LOM}\right|_{ED} = \left.\frac{\partial ED}{\partial LOM}\right|_{AI} \times \left.\frac{\partial LYE}{\partial ED}\right|_{FB} = 100\times(-.0031)\times(.0645) = -.0200$$

on the average earnings levels of arriving male immigrants. That is, their average earnings levels are reduced by 2.0 percent. The corresponding calculation for women yields an estimated reduction of 2.1 percent.

But changes in the overall inflow level of immigration also have an effect on the average age of arriving immigrants. The effect operating through age of arriving immigrants is given by

$$\left.\frac{\partial LYE}{\partial LOM}\right|_{AGE} = \left.\frac{\partial AGE}{\partial LOM}\right|_{AI} \times \left.\frac{\partial LYE}{\partial EXP}\right|_{FB}, \tag{2}$$

where EXP is now years of labour market work experience of landing immigrants. This effect depends, in turn, on two terms: how immigration levels affect the average age of arriving immigrants (the first term), and how age or amount of work experience affects immigrants' expected earnings (the second term). The first term is given by the estimation results in the first column of Table A-2, as specified in Appendix B:

$$\left.\frac{\partial AGE}{\partial LOM}\right|_{AI} = -.00290$$

The second term, derived in Appendix C, is

$$\left.\frac{\partial LYE}{\partial EXP}\right|_{FB} = .00479 \text{ for males and } \left.\frac{\partial LYE}{\partial EXP}\right|_{FB} = .00241 \text{ for females.}$$

Consequently, the estimated effect of increasing the total level of immigration by 100,000 immigrants per year is given by

$$\left.\frac{\partial LYE}{\partial LOM}\right|_{AGE} = \left.\frac{\partial AGE}{\partial LOM}\right|_{AI} \times \left.\frac{\partial LYE}{\partial EXP}\right|_{FB} = 100\times(-.00290)\times(.00479) = -.00139$$

on the average earnings levels of arriving male immigrants. That is, their average earnings levels are reduced by 0.14 percent. The corresponding calculation for female immigrants is an estimated reduction of 0.070 percent.

Finally, the effect of changes in immigrant inflow levels on immigrant earnings levels can operate through the degree of fluency in either English or French of arriving immigrants:

$$\left.\frac{\partial LYE}{\partial LOM}\right|_{LF} = \left.\frac{\partial PLF}{\partial LOM}\right|_{AI} \times \left.\frac{\partial LYE}{\partial PLF}\right|_{FB} , \tag{3}$$

where PLF is the proportion of arriving immigrants said to be fluent in either English or French. Again, this operates through two terms: how immigration levels affect the average (as a proportion between 0 and 1) of arriving immigrants, and how host-country language fluency affects immigrants' expected earnings. The first term is given by estimation results in the first column of Table A-3, as detailed in Appendix B:

$$\left.\frac{\partial PLF}{\partial LOM}\right|_{AI} = -.00011.$$

The second term is explained in Appendix C and takes on values

$$\left.\frac{\partial LYE}{\partial PLF}\right|_{FB} = 1.1871 \text{ for males and } \left.\frac{\partial LYE}{\partial PLF}\right|_{FB} = 1.1078 \text{ for females.}$$

Thus, combining these results,

$$\left.\frac{\partial LYE}{\partial LOM}\right|_{LF} = \left.\frac{\partial PLF}{\partial LOM}\right|_{AI} \times \left.\frac{\partial LYE}{\partial PLF}\right|_{FB}$$

$$= (-.00011) \times (1.1871)$$

$$= -.0001306$$

for males and $-.0001219$ for females. That is, immigrant males' average (log) earnings levels for an increase in the total level of immigration by 100 thousand immigrants per year are reduced by .013, or by 1.3 percent, and those of immigrant females by 1.2 percent.

The combined effect from equations (1), (2), and (3) of increasing the overall level of immigration by 100,000 a year operating through the ED, AGE, and LF channels is given by the sum

$$\frac{\partial LYE}{\partial LOM} = \left.\frac{\partial LYE}{\partial LOM}\right|_{ED} + \left.\frac{\partial LYE}{\partial LOM}\right|_{AGE} + \left.\frac{\partial LYE}{\partial LOM}\right|_{LF} \qquad (4)$$

For females, this comes to $-.0339$ (or a 3.39 percent reduction); and for males $-.0345$ (or a 3.45 percent reduction) in entry earnings levels, with the education channel the strongest component, the age or experience channel by far the weakest, and the language fluency channel about 60 percent of the strength of the education channel.

The Economic Class Share (ECS)

Calculations of the effects of changes in the share of immigrants arriving in the Economic Class (ECS) proceed analogously to those for LOM. Again, there are three channels through which changes in ECS operate — the education, age, and language fluency of arriving immigrants.

The effect of changes in ECS on the entry earnings of immigrants operating through the average years-of-education channel is

$$\left.\frac{\partial LYE}{\partial ECS}\right|_{ED} = \left.\frac{\partial ED}{\partial ECS}\right|_{AI} \times \left.\frac{\partial LYE}{\partial ED}\right|_{FB}. \qquad (5)$$

The second term in this expression was calculated in Appendix C as .0680 for females and .0645 for males. For the first term in the expression, the effect of a change in the Economic Class share of immigrants on the average education level of arriving immigrants is given by the estimation results in the first column of Appendix Table A-1, as detailed in Appendix B. In this case,

$$\left.\frac{\partial ED}{\partial ECS}\right|_{AI} = (.01)(2.639)-.00051$$

$$= .0259$$

Consequently, the estimated effect of increasing the Economic Class share by, say, 10 percentage points is given by

$$\left.\frac{\partial LYE}{\partial ECS}\right|_{ED} = \left.\frac{\partial ED}{\partial ECS}\right|_{AI} \times \left.\frac{\partial LYE}{\partial ED}\right|_{FB} = 10\times(.0259)\times(.0680)=.0176$$

on the average earnings of immigrant females. That is, their average earnings levels increase by about 1.8 percent. The corresponding calculation for males yields an estimated increase of .0167, or about 1.7 percent.

Changes in the Economic Class share of immigration also have an effect through the average age of arriving immigrants:

$$\left.\frac{\partial LYE}{\partial ECS}\right|_{AGE} = \left.\frac{\partial AGE}{\partial ECS}\right|_{AI} \times \left.\frac{\partial LYE}{\partial EXP}\right|_{FB}. \tag{6}$$

Once again, the second term of this expression was calculated in Appendix C as .00241 for females and .00479 for males. The first term in the expression was calculated directly from the coefficients of the first column of Table A-2 as −.0273 (see Appendix B). Consequently, the estimated effect of increasing the Economic Class share again by 10 percentage points through its effect on average age of arriving immigrants is

$$\left.\frac{\partial LYE}{\partial ECS}\right|_{AGE} = \left.\frac{\partial AGE}{\partial ECS}\right|_{AI} \times \left.\frac{\partial LYE}{\partial EXP}\right|_{FB} = 10\times(-.0273)\times(.00479) = -.00131$$

for immigrant males. That is, their average earnings levels are estimated to fall by about 0.13 percent. The corresponding calculation for females yields an estimated decline of .00066, or about 0.07 percent.

Thirdly, the effect of changes in the Economic Class share on immigrants' earnings levels can operate through the degree of fluency in either English or French of arriving immigrants:

$$\frac{\partial LYE}{\partial ECS}\bigg|_{LF} = \frac{\partial PLF}{\partial ECS}\bigg|_{AI} \times \frac{\partial LYE}{\partial PLF}\bigg|_{FB}. \qquad (7)$$

The second term in this expression was calculated above as 1.108 for females and 1.187 for males. The first term is given by estimation results in the first column of Table A-3, as specified in Appendix B:

$$\frac{\partial PLF}{\partial ECS}\bigg|_{AI} = (.01)(0.2605)+.00246$$

$$= .005065.$$

Combining these effects,

$$\frac{\partial LYE}{\partial ECS}\bigg|_{LF} = (.005065)\times(1.1817)$$

$$= .006013$$

for immigrant males and .005612 for females. So, a 10 percentage point increase in the Economic Class share of immigration is estimated to raise the average earnings levels of landing female immigrants by 5.6 percent and those of landing male immigrants by 6.0 percent.

The combined effect of increasing the Economic Class share by 10 percentage points operating through the ED, AGE, and LF channels is thus the sum

$$\frac{\partial LYE}{\partial ECS} = \frac{\partial LYE}{\partial ECS}\bigg|_{ED} + \frac{\partial LYE}{\partial ECS}\bigg|_{AGE} \times \frac{\partial LYE}{\partial ECS}\bigg|_{LF}. \qquad (8)$$

For females, this comes to .0730 (or a 7.3 percent increase), and for males .0755 (or a 7.5 percent increase) in entry earnings levels, with the language fluency channel component being by far the largest, the age or experience channel very minor, and the education channel in between.

Point System Weights (PSW)

Point System Weight on Education (PSWED)

Changing point system weights operates directly only on principal applicants, the group whose skills the system actually evaluates. In our analysis, each skill weight within the point system has a direct effect on that respective skill outcome for arriving immigrants. So, if PSW_{ED} is the maximum point system weight given for years of education, then

$$\frac{\partial LYE}{\partial PSW_{ED}} = \frac{\partial ED}{\partial PSW_{ED}}\bigg|_{PA} \times \frac{\partial LYE}{\partial ED}\bigg|_{FB}. \qquad (9)$$

The first term in this expression, from the second column of Table A-1, is .03534. The second term was calculated in Appendix C to be .0645 for immigrant males and .0680 for females. Consequently, the effect of increasing the maximum weight on years of education in the point system by 10 percentage points is

$$\frac{\partial LYE}{\partial PSW_{ED}} = \frac{\partial ED}{\partial PSW_{ED}}\bigg|_{PA} \times \frac{\partial LYE}{\partial ED}\bigg|_{FB} = 10\times(.03534)\times(.0645) = .02279$$

on the average earnings of male principal applicants, or an increase in earnings of about 2.3 percent. Similarly, for female principal applicants, the estimate is .02403, or about a 2.4 percent increase.

Point System Weight on Age at Arrival (PSWAGE)

In the case of changing the maximum point system weight given to the principal applicant's age at arrival, the relevant calculation involves

$$\frac{\partial LYE}{\partial PSW_{AGE}} = \frac{\partial AGE}{\partial PSW_{AGE}}\bigg|_{PA} \times \frac{\partial LYE}{\partial EXP}\bigg|_{FB}. \qquad (10)$$

The first term in this expression, taken from the second column of Table A-2, is −.01707. Again, the second term was calculated in Appendix C for immigrant males as .00479 and for females as .00241. Consequently, the effect on the average entry earnings of arriving male immigrants of increasing the maximum weight on age at arrival of principal applicants by 10 percentage points is

$$\frac{\partial LYE}{\partial PSW_{AGE}} = \frac{\partial AGE}{\partial PSW_{AGE}}\bigg|_{PA} \times \frac{\partial LYE}{\partial EXP}\bigg|_{FB} = 10\times(-.01707)\times(.00479) = -.0008177,$$

or about a .08 percent decrease in average earnings. The corresponding estimate for female principal applicants is −.0003825, or about a .04 percent reduction in earnings.

Point System Weight on Language Fluency (PSWLF)

The effect of changing the maximum point system weight on the principal applicant's fluency in either English or French is given by

$$\frac{\partial LYE}{\partial PSW_{LF}} = \frac{\partial PLF}{\partial PSW_{LF}}\bigg|_{PA} \times \frac{\partial LYE}{\partial PLF}\bigg|_{FB}. \tag{11}$$

The first term in this expression, taken from the second column of Table A-3, is .00091. The second term was calculated in Appendix C for immigrant males as 1.187 and for females as 1.108. Consequently, the effect on the average entry earnings of arriving male immigrants of increasing the maximum weight on language fluency at arrival of principal applicants by 10 percentage points is

$$\frac{\partial LYE}{\partial PSW_{LF}} = \frac{\partial PLF}{\partial PSW_{LF}}\bigg|_{PA} \times \frac{\partial LYE}{\partial PLF}\bigg|_{FB} = 10\times(.00091)\times(1.187) = .0108,$$

or about a 1.1 percent increase in average earnings. The corresponding estimate for female principal applicants is .0101, or about a 1.0 percent increase in earnings.

Unemployment Rate Effects on Earnings

The Canadian and US unemployment rates have a highly statistically significant effect on the average skills levels of arriving immigrants and hence on their average entry earnings levels.

Canadian Unemployment Rate Effects on Earnings

We look at direct effects on the average earnings of principal applicants. Again, the effects of the unemployment rate operate through all three skills outcome variables: education, age at arrival, and language fluency of landing principal applicants. So, if UR_C is the Canadian unemployment rate, then the effect of changes in this rate on average entry earnings operating through its effect on immigrants' education level is given by

$$\left.\frac{\partial LYE}{\partial UR_C}\right|_{ED} = \left.\frac{\partial ED}{\partial UR_C}\right|_{PA} \times \left.\frac{\partial LYE}{\partial ED}\right|_{FB} \tag{12}$$

The first term captures the effect of unemployment rate changes in Canada on the education level of arriving immigrants; from the second column in Appendix Table A-1, it is −.0967. The second term represents the effect of an additional year of education on the average (log) earnings of immigrants in the Canadian labour market. This was calculated in Appendix C as .0645 for immigrant males and .0680 for immigrant females. Consequently, the estimated effect of a 3 percentage point rise in the Canadian unemployment on the average earnings of arriving principal applicants through its effect on immigrants' average education level is given by

$$\left.\frac{\partial LYE}{\partial UR_C}\right|_{ED} = 3 \times (-.0967) \times (.0645) = -.0187,$$

or a 1.9 percent reduction in earnings for immigrant males. The corresponding reduction for females is −.0197 or by 2.0 percent.

The analogous effect operating through the age channel is given by

$$\left.\frac{\partial LYE}{\partial UR_C}\right|_{AGE} = \left.\frac{\partial AGE}{\partial UR_C}\right|_{PA} \times \left.\frac{\partial LYE}{\partial EXP}\right|_{FB}. \tag{13}$$

The first term, obtained from the second column of Table A-2, is .5144. The second term was calculated in Appendix C as .00479 for immigrant males and .00241 for females. Thus, the estimated effect of a 3 percentage point rise in the Canadian unemployment rate corresponds to an increase in principal applicants' average earnings via its effect on age at arrival of

$$\left.\frac{\partial LYE}{\partial UR_C}\right|_{AGE} = 3\times(.5144)\times(.00479) = .00739,$$

or just 0.74 percent. The corresponding figure for females is .00372, or a 0.37 percent increase.

The effect operating through the language fluency channel then is given by

$$\left.\frac{\partial LYE}{\partial UR_C}\right|_{LF} = \left.\frac{\partial PLF}{\partial UR_C}\right|_{PA}\times\left.\frac{\partial LYE}{\partial PLF}\right|_{FB}. \tag{14}$$

The first term, obtained from the second column of Table A-3, is .04281. The second term was calculated in Appendix C as 1.1871 for immigrant males and 1.1078 for females. So the estimated effect of a 3 percentage point rise in the Canadian unemployment rate via its effect on language fluency is an increase in the average entry earnings of principal applicants of

$$\left.\frac{\partial LYE}{\partial UR_C}\right|_{LF} = 3\times(.04281)\times(1.1871) = .15246,$$

or 15.2 percent. The corresponding figure for women is .14227 or a 14.2 percent increase.

The total effect of a 3 percentage point rise in the Canadian unemployment rate operating through all three skill channels is

$$\frac{\partial LYE}{\partial UR_C} = \left.\frac{\partial LYE}{\partial UR_C}\right|_{ED} + \left.\frac{\partial LYE}{\partial UR_C}\right|_{AGE} + \left.\frac{\partial LYE}{\partial UR_C}\right|_{LF}$$

$$= -.0187+.0074+.1525$$

$$= .1412$$

for male principal applicants and .1263 for females.

US Unemployment Rate Effects on Earnings

Here, the calculations proceed analogously to those above, except that now the US unemployment rate coefficients are drawn from Appendix Tables A-1, A-2, and A-3. To summarize the calculations for the effects of a 3 percentage point rise in the US unemployment rate on the average entry earnings of landing principal applicants in Canada:

$$\left.\frac{\partial LYE}{\partial UR_{US}}\right|_{ED} = \left.\frac{\partial ED}{\partial UR_{US}}\right|_{PA} \times \left.\frac{\partial LYE}{\partial ED}\right|_{FB} = (.1958) \times (.0645) \times 3 = .0379 \text{ for males} \tag{15}$$

$$= (.1958) \times (.0680) \times 3 = .0399 \text{ for females.}$$

$$\left.\frac{\partial LYE}{\partial UR_{US}}\right|_{AGE} = \left.\frac{\partial AGE}{\partial UR_{US}}\right|_{PA} \times \left.\frac{\partial LYE}{\partial EXP}\right|_{FB} = (-.3926) \times (.00479) \times 3 = -.00564 \text{ for males} \tag{16}$$

$$= (-.3926) \times (.00241) \times 3 = -.00284 \text{ for females.}$$

$$\left.\frac{\partial LYE}{\partial UR_{US}}\right|_{LF} = \left.\frac{\partial PLF}{\partial UR_{US}}\right|_{PA} \times \left.\frac{\partial LYE}{\partial PLF}\right|_{FB} = (-.04317) \times (1.1871) \times 3 = -.1537 \text{ for males} \tag{17}$$

$$= (-.04317) \times (1.1078) \times 3 = -.1434 \text{ for females.}$$

The total effect, then, is the sum of these three effects: $-.1214$ for males and $-.1063$ for females.

Bibliography

Abbott, Michael, G., and Charles M. Beach. 2011. "Do Admission Category and Economic Recessions Affect Immigrant Earnings?" Paper prepared for the Institute for Research on Public Policy, Montreal, September; forthcoming as an IRPP study.

Akbari, Ather. 1989. "The Benefits of Immigrants to Canada: Evidence on Tax and Public Services." *Canadian Public Policy* 15 (4): 424–35.

———. (1995). "The Impact of Immigrants on Public Treasury Circa 1990." In *Diminishing Returns: The Economics of Canada's Recent Immigration Policy*, edited by Don J. DeVoretz. Toronto: C.D. Howe Institute.

Alboim, Naomi, Ross Finnie and Ronald Meng. 2005. "The Discounting of Immigrants' Skills in Canada: Evidence and Policy Recommendations." *IRPP Choices*, Institute for Research on Public Policy 11(2).

Alboim, Naomi, and Maytree Foundation. 2009. "Adjusting the Balance-Fixing Canada's Economic Immigration Policies." Toronto: Maytree Foundation. Available at www.maytree.com/policy.

Auditor General of Canada. 2009. *Report to the House of Commons*. Ottawa: Office of the Auditor General of Canada.

Aydemir, Abdurrahman. 2003. "Effects of Business Cycles on the Labour Market Assimilation of Immigrants." In *Canadian Immigration Policy for the 21st Century*, edited by Charles M. Beach, Alan G. Green, and Jeffrey G. Reitz. Kingston, ON: McGill-Queen's University Press.

Aydemir, Abdurrahman, and Mikal Skuterud. 2005. "Explaining the Deteriorating Entry Earnings of Canada's Immigrant Cohorts, 1966-2000." *Canadian Journal of Economics* 38 (2): 641–71.

———. 2008. "The Immigrant Wage Differential within and across Establishments." *Industrial and Labor Relations Review* 61 (3): 334–52.

Baker, Michael, and Dwayne Benjamin. 1994. "The Performance of Immigrants in the Canadian Labor Market." *Journal of Labor Economics* 12 (3): 369–405.

Banerjee, Robin, and William B.P. Robson. 2009. *Faster, Younger, Richer? The Fond Hope and Sobering Reality of Immigration's Impact on Canada's Demographic and Economic Future*. C.D. Howe Institute, Commentary 291. Toronto: C.D. Howe Institute.

Beach, Charles M., Alan G. Green, and Christopher Worswick. 2008. "Impacts of the Point System and Immigration Policy Levers on Skill Characteristics of Canadian Immigrants." In *Immigration: Trends, Consequences and Prospects for the United States*, Research in Labor Economics 27, edited by Barry R. Chiswick. Amsterdam: Elsevier JAI Press.

Beaudry, Paul, and David A. Green. 2000. "Cohort Patterns in Canadian Earnings: Assessing the Role of Skill Premia in Inequality Trends." *Canadian Journal of Economics* 33 (4): 907–36.

Becker, Gary. 1964. *Human Capital*. New York: Columbia University Press for the National Bureau of Economic Research.

Benjamin, Dwayne, Morley Gunderson, Thomas Lemieux, and W. Craig Riddell. 2007. *Labour Market Economics: Theory, Evidence and Policy in Canada*, 6th ed. Toronto: McGraw-Hill Ryerson.

Bloom, David E., Gilles Grenier, and Morley Gunderson. 1995. "The Changing Labour Market Position of Canadian Immigrants." *Canadian Journal of Economics* 28 (4): 987–1005.

Bonikowska, Aneta, David A. Green, and W. Craig Riddell. 2008. "Literacy and the Labour Market: Cognitive Skills and Immigrant Earnings." *International Adult Literacy Survey*. Cat. 89-552-M No. 020. Ottawa: Statistics Canada.

———. 2010. "Immigrant Skills and Immigrant Outcomes under a Selection System: The Canadian Experience." Unpublished paper.

Bonikowska, Aneta, Feng Hou, and Garnett Picot. 2008. "A Canada-U.S. Comparison of Labour Market Outcomes." Statistics Canada Analytical Studies. Ottawa: Statistics Canada.

Bonin, Holger. 2006. "Cost-Benefit Analysis of Immigration: Foreigners Living in Germany Are Net Contributors to Public Budgets." *IZA Compact* (Institute for the Study of Labor) (December), pp. 4–7.

Borjas, George J. 1985. "Assimilation, Change in Cohort Quality, and the Earnings of Immigrants." *Journal of Labor Economics* 3 (4): 463–89.

———. 1993. "Immigration Policy, National Origin, and Immigrant Skills: A Comparison of Canada and the United States." In *Small Differences That Matter: Labor Markets and Income Maintenance in Canada and the United States*, edited by David Card and Richard B. Freeman. Chicago: University of Chicago Press.

———. 1995a. "The Economic Benefits from Immigration." *Journal of Economic Perspectives* 9 (2): 3-22.

———. 1995b. "Assimilation and Changes in Cohort Quality Revisited: What Happened to Immigrant Earnings in the 1980s?" *Journal of Economics* 13 (2): 201–45.

———. 1999. *Heaven's Door: Immigration Policy and the American Economy*. Princeton, NJ: Princeton University Press.

———. 2003. "The Labor Demand Curve Is Downward Sloping: Re-examining the Impact of Immigration on the Labor Market." *Quarterly Journal of Economics* 118 (4): 1135–74.

Boudarbat, Brahim, Maude Boulet, and Nong Zhu. 2010. "Labour Market Participation and Employment Income among Immigrants in Quebec Compared with Those in the Rest of Canada." *Our Diverse Cities: Immigration and Diversity*, No.7, The Metropolis Project, Citizenship and Immigration Canada: pp.56-62.

Boyd, Monica. 2009. "Language at Work: The Impact of Linguistic Enclaves on Immigrant Economic Integration." CLSRN Working Paper 41. Canadian Labour Market and Skills Researcher Network.

Card, David. 2009. "Immigration and Inequality." *American Economic Review: Papers and Proceedings* 99 (2): 1–21.

Carter, Tom, Manish Pandey, and James Townsend. 2010. "The Manitoba Provincial Nominee Program: Attraction, Integration and Retention of Immigrants." IRPP Study 10. Montreal: Institute for Research on Public Policy.

Chiswick, Barry R. 1978. "The Effect of Americanization on the Earnings of Foreign-born Men." *Journal of Political Economy* 86 (5): 239–49.

Chiswick, Barry R., and Paul W. Miller. 2001. "A Model of Destination-Language Acquisition: Application to Male Immigrants in Canada." *Demography* 38 (3): 391–401.

———. 2007. *The Economics of Language: International Analyses*. New York: Routledge.

———. 2008. "Modeling Immigrant Language Skills." In *Immigration: Trends, Consequences and Prospects for the United States*, Research in Labor Economics 27, edited by Barry R. Chiswick. Amsterdam: Elsevier JAI Press.

———. 2010. "An Explanation for the Lower Payoff to Schooling for Immigrants in the Canadian Labour Market." In *Canadian Immigration: Economic Evidence for a Dynamic Policy Environment*, edited by Ted McDonald, Elizabeth Ruddick, Arthur Sweetman, and Christopher Worswick. Kingston, ON: McGill-Queen's University Press.

Christofides, Louis N., and Robert Swidinsky. 2010. "The Economic Returns to the Knowledge and Use of a Second Official Language: English in Quebec and French in the Rest-of-Canada." *Canadian Public Policy* 36 (2): 137–58.

Citizenship and Immigration Canada. 1994. "Into the 21st Century: A Strategy for Immigration and Citizenship." Ottawa: Supply and Services Canada.

———. 1999. *Citizenship and Immigration Statistics 1996*, Cat. No. MP22-1/1996. Ottawa.

———. 2004. *Recent Immigrant Outcomes — 2004*. Ottawa. Available online at http://www.cic.gc.ca, accessed April 18, 2010.

———. 2009. *Facts and Figures 2008 — Immigration Overview: Permanent and Temporary Residents*. Ottawa.

———. 2011. *Facts and Figures 2011: Permanent and Temporary Residents*. Available on the CIC website at: www.cic.gc.ca/english/resources/statistics/facts 2011/. Accessed June 20, 2011.

Conference Board of Canada. 2009. "Immigrant-Friendly Businesses: Effective Practices for Attracting, Integrating and Retaining Immigrants in Canadian Workplaces." Ottawa.

———. 2010. "Immigrants as Innovators: Boosting Canada's Global Competitiveness." Ottawa.

Dolin, Benjamin, and Margaret Young. 2002. "Canada's Immigration Policy (revised October 2002)." Depository Service Program BP-190E. Available online at http://www.collectionscanada.gc.ca/webarchives/20061219071534/, accessed April 22, 2010.

Drummond, Don. 2009. "The Rising Importance of Immigrants." Presentation slides from a talk given on November 27.

Drummond, D., and F. Fong. 2010. "An Economics Perspective on Canadian Immigration." *Policy Options* 31 (July-August), pp. 28–34.

Dustmann, C., and F. Fabbri. 1995. "Language Proficiency and Labour Market Performance of Immigrants in the U.K." *Economic Journal* 113 (489): 695–717.

Dustmann, Christian, Albrecht Glitz, and Thomasso Frattini. 2008. "The Labour Market Impact of Immigration." Discussion Paper 11/08. London: University College, Centre for Research and Analysis of Migration.

Dustmann, Christian, Tim Hatton, and Ian Preston. 2005. "The Labour Market Effects of Immigration." *Economic Journal* 115 (507): F297–F299.

Dustmann, C., and A. van Soest. 2002. "Language and the Earnings of Immigrants." *Industrial and Labor Relations Review* 55 (3): 473-492.

Economic Council of Canada. 1991. *Economic and Social Impacts of Immigration.* Ottawa: Supply and Services Canada.

Ferrer, Ana, David A. Green, and W. Craig Riddell. 2006. "The Effect of Literacy on Immigrant Earnings." *Journal of Human Resources* 41 (2): 380–410.

Ferrer, Ana, and W. Craig Riddell. 2008. "Education, Credentials, and Immigrant Earnings." *Canadian Journal of Economics* 41 (1): 186–216.

Frenette, Marc, and René Morrisette. 2003. "Will They Ever Converge? Earnings of Immigrant and Canadian-Born Workers Over the Last Two Decades." Analytical Studies Research Paper Series 215. Ottawa: Statistics Canada.

Gilmore, Jason. 2008. *The Canadian Immigrant Labour Market in 2006: Analysis by Region or Country of Birth.* Cat. 71-606-X2008002. Ottawa: Statistics Canada.

Goldmann, Gustave, Arthur Sweetman, and Casey Warman. 2009. "The Economic Returns on New Immigrants' Human Capital: The Impact of Occupational Matching." CLSRN Working Paper 21. Canadian Labour Market and Skills Researcher Network.

Grady, Patrick. 2010. "An Analysis of the Underlying Causes of the Poor Performance of Recent Immigrants Using the 2006 Census PUMF and Some Observations on Their Implications for Immigration Policy." Working Paper 2010-2. Ottawa: Global Economics.

Grant, Mary L. 1999. "Evidence of New Immigrant Assimilation in Canada." *Canadian Journal of Economics* 32 (4): 930–55.

Green, Alan G. 1976. *Immigration and the Postwar Canadian Economy.* Toronto: Macmillan of Canada.

―――. 1995. "A Comparison of Canadian and US Immigration Policy in the Twentieth Century." In *Diminishing Returns: The Economics of Canada's Recent Immigration Policy*, edited by Don J. DeVoretz. Toronto: C.D. Howe Institute.

―――. 2003. "What is the Role of Immigration in Canada's Future? In *Canadian Immigration Policy for the 21ˢᵗ Century*, edited by Charles M. Beach, Alan G. Green and Jeffrey G. Reitz. John Deutsch Institute. Kingston: McGill-Queen's University Press.

Green, Alan G., and David A. Green.1995. "Canadian Immigration Policy: The Effectiveness of the Point System and Other Instruments." *Canadian Journal of Economics*, vol. 28(4b), pp. 1006-1041.

Green, Alan G., and David A. Green. 1999. "The Economic Goals of Canada's Immigration Policy: Past and Present." *Canadian Public Policy* 26 (4): 425–51.

Green, David A. 1999. "Immigrant Occupational Attainment: Assimilation and Adjustment over Time." *Journal of Labor Economics* 17 (1): 49–79.

Green, David A., and Christopher Worswick. 2002. "Earnings of Immigrant Men in Canada: The Roles of Labour Market Entry Effects and Returns to Foreign Experience." Paper presented at the John Deutsch Institute Conference on "Canadian Immigration Policy for the 21st Century," Queen's University, Kingston, ON, October 18–19.

―――. 2004. "Immigrant Earnings Profiles in the Presence of Human Capital Investment: Measuring Cohort and Macro Effects." Working Paper 04/13. London: Institute for Fiscal Studies.

―――. 2010a. "Entry Earnings of Immigrant Men in Canada: The Roles of Labour Market Entry Effects and Returns to Foreign Experience." In *Canadian Immigration: Economic Evidence for a Dynamic Policy Environment*, edited by Ted McDonald, Elizabeth Ruddick, Arthur Sweetman, and Christopher Worswick. Kingston, ON: McGill-Queen's University Press.

―――. 2010b. "Immigrant Earnings Profiles in the Presence of Human Capital Investment: Measuring Cohort and Macro Effects." Unpublished.

Guillemette, Yvan, and William B.P. Robson. 2006. "No Elixir for Youth: Immigration Cannot Keep Canada Young." *Backgrounder* 96. Toronto: C.D. Howe Institute.

Hawkins, Freda. 1972. *Canada and Immigration: Public Policy and Public Concern.* Montreal; Kingston, ON: McGill-Queen's University Press.

Hawthorne, Lesley Anne. 2005. "'Picking Winners': The Recent Transformation of Australia's Skilled Migration Policy." *International Migration Review* 39 (3): 663–96.

———. 2008. "The Impact of Economic Selection Policy on Labour Market Outcomes for Degree-Qualified Migrants in Canada and Australia." *IRPP Choices* 14 (5).

Health and Welfare Canada. 1989. *Charting Canada's Future: A Report of the Demographic Review.* Ottawa: Health and Welfare Canada.

Hou, Feng. 2004. "Recent Immigration and the Formation of Visible Minority Neighborhoods in Canada's Large Cities." Analytical Studies Research Paper Series 221. Ottawa: Statistics Canada.

———. 2010. "Entry Earnings of Canada's Immigrants over the Past Quarter Century: The Roles of Changing Characteristics and Returns to Skills." CLSRN Working Paper 63. Canadian Labour Market and Skills Researcher Network.

Hou, Feng, and John Myles. 2007. "The Changing Role of Education in the Marriage Market: Assortive Marriage in Canada and the United States Since the 1970s." Analytical Studies Research Paper Series 299. Ottawa. Statistics Canada.

Hou, Feng, and Garnett Picot. 2010. "Immigrant Entry Earnings over the Past Quarter Century: Re-examining the Roles of Changing Characteristics and Returns to Skills." Unpublished.

Hum, Derek, and Wayne Simpson. 1999. "Wage Opportunities for Visible Minorities in Canada." *Canadian Public Policy* 25 (3): 379–94.

———. 2004. "Economic Integration of Immigrants to Canada: A Short Survey." *Canadian Journal of Urban Research* 13 (1): 46–61.

Johnson, George E. 1980. "The Labor Market Effects of Immigration." *Industrial and Labor Relations Review* 33 (3): 331–41.

Kato, Takao, and Chad Sparber. 2010. "Quotas and Quality: The Effect of H-1B Visa Restrictions on the Pool of Prospective Undergraduate Students from Abroad." Discussion Paper 10/10. London: University College, Centre for Research and Analysis of Migration.

Lewis, Nathaniel M. 2010. "A Decade Later: Assessing Successes and Challenges in Manitoba's Provincial Immigrant Nominee Program." *Canadian Public Policy* 36(2): 241-264.

Little, Matthew. 2010. "Group calls for immigration overhaul." *Epoch Times*, Toronto edition, September 30, pp. 1–2.

Mahony, Jill. 2010. "Who will succeed and by what measure?" *Globe and Mail*, October 6, p. A16.

Martin, Philip. 2010. "Temporary Worker Programs: US and Global Experiences." In *Canadian Issues: Temporary Foreign Workers* (Spring), pp. 122–27.

McBride, Stephen, and Arthur Sweetman. 2003. "Immigrant and Non-Immigrant Earnings by Post-Secondary Field of Study." In *Canadian Immigration Policy for the 21st Century*, edited by Charles M. Beach, Alan G. Green, and Jeffrey G. Reitz. Kingston, ON: McGill-Queen's University Press.

McDonald, James Ted, and Christopher Worswick. 1997. "Unemployment Incidence of Immigrant Men in Canada." *Canadian Public Policy* 23 (3): 353–71.

———. 1998. "The Earnings of Immigrant Men in Canada: Job Tenure, Cohort, and Macroeconomic Conditions." *Industrial and Labor Relations Review,* 51(3): 465-482.

McWhinney, Mike. 1998. "A Selection Criteria Chronology, 1967–1997: Critical Changes in Definitions, the Point System and Priority Processing." Ottawa: Citizenship and Immigration Canada, Strategic Research and Review Branch. Unpublished.

Mincer, Jacob. 1974. *Schooling, Experience, and Earnings.* New York: Columbia University Press for the National Bureau of Economic Research.

Nadeau, Serge. 2010. "Another Look at the Francophone Wage Gap in Canada: Public and Private Sectors, Quebec and Outside Quebec." *Canadian Public Policy* 36 (2): 159–80.

Nadeau, Serge, and Aylin Seckin. 2010. "The Immigrant Wage Gap in Canada: Quebec and the Rest of Canada." *Canadian Public Policy* 36 (3): 265–85.

Nakache, Delphine, and Paula J. Kinoshita. 2010. "The Canadian Temporary Foreign Worker Program: Do Short-Term Economic Needs Prevail Over Human Rights Concerns?" Study No. 5 for the Institute for Research on Public Policy.

OECD (Organisation for Economic Co-Operation and Development). 2008.

International Migration Outlook 2008. Paris.

Pandey, Manish, and James Townsend. 2010. "Provincial Nominee Programs: An Evaluation of the Earnings and Retention Rates of Nominees." Unpublished.

Paperny, Anna Mehler. 2010. "Failure to tap into immigrants' skills costs billions." *Globe and Mail*, June 10, p. A1.

Pencavel, John. 1998. "Assortive Mating by Schooling and Working Behavior of Husbands and Wives." *American Economic Review*. 88(2): 326-29.

Peri, Giovanni, and Francisco Requena-Silvente. 2010. "The Trade Creation Effect of Immigrants: Evidence from the Remarkable Case of Spain." *Canadian Journal of Economics* 43 (4): 1433–59.

Picot, Garnett. 2010. "Using Recent Immigration Research to Address Questions Posed for Session." Presentation to an Institute for Research on Public Policy conference on "Canada's Immigration Policy: Reconciling Labour Market Needs and Longer-Term Goals," Ottawa, May 25–26.

Picot, Garnett, and Feng Hou. 2009. "Immigrant Characteristics, the IT Bust, and Their Effect on Entry Earnings of Immigrants." Analytical Studies Research Paper 315. Ottawa: Statistics Canada.

Picot, Garnett, and Arthur Sweetman. 2005. "The Deteriorating Economic Welfare of Immigrants and Possible Causes: Update 2005." Analytical Studies Research Paper Series 262. Ottawa: Statistics Canada.

Reitz, Jeffrey G. 2001. "Immigrant Success in the Knowledge Economy: Institutional Changes and the Immigrant Experience in Canada, 1970-1995." *Journal of Social Issues* 57 (3): 579–613.

———. 2004. "Canada: Immigration and Nation-Building in the Transition to a Knowledge Economy." In *Controlling Immigration: A Global Perspective*, edited by Wayne A. Cornelius, Takeyuki Tsuda, Philip L. Martin, and James F. Hollifield. Stanford, CA: Stanford University Press.

———. 2005. "Tapping Immigrants' Skills: New Directions for Canadian Immigration Policy in the Knowledge Economy." *IRPP Choices* 11 (February).

———. 2006. "Recent Trends in the Integration of Immigrants in the Canadian Labour Market: A Multi-Disciplinary Synthesis of Research." Unpublished.

———. 2007. "Immigrant Employment Success in Canada, Part ii: Understanding the Decline." *Journal of International Migration and Integration* 8 (1): 37–62.

_____. 2010. "Selecting Immigrants for the Short Term: Is it Smart in the Long Run?" *Policy Options*, Institute for Research on Public Policy 31 (July-August) pp. 12-16.

Schaafsma, Joseph, and Arthur Sweetman. 2001. "Immigrant Earnings: Age at Immigration." *Canadian Journal of Economics* 34 (4): 1066–99.

Siemiatycki, Myer, ed. 2005. *Canadian Issues: Immigration and the Intersections of Diversity* (Spring).

Simon, Julian L. 1989. *The Economic Consequences of Immigration*. Oxford: Blackwell Publishers.

Skills Research Initiative. 2008. "International Mobility of Highly Skilled Workers: A Synthesis of Key Findings and Policy Implications." Ottawa: Industry Canada and Human Resources and Social Development Canada.

Skuterud, Mikal, and Mingcui Su. 2009. "Immigrant Wage Assimilation and the Return to Foreign and Host-Country Sources of Human Capital." CLSRN Working Paper 30. Canadian Labour Market and Skills Researcher Network.

Smith, James P. 2006. "Immigrants and the Labor Market." *Journal of Labor Economics* 24 (2): 203–34.

Smith, James P., and Barry Edmonston, eds. 1997. *The New Americans: Economic, Demographic, and Fiscal Effects of Immigration*. Washington, DC: National Academy Press.

Statistics Canada. 2007. *Immigration in Canada: A Portrait of the Foreign-born Population, 2006 Census*. Cat. 97-557-XIE. Ottawa.

_____. 2008a. "Historical Statistical Supplement 2007/2008." *Canadian Economic Observer*, Cat. 11-210-XPB.

_____. 2008b. *Canada's Changing Labour Force, 2006 Census*. Cat. 97-559-X. Ottawa.

_____. 2010. *Canadian Economic Observer*, Cat. 11-010 (February).

Studin, Irvin. 2010. "Canada — Population 100 Million." *Global Brief*, June 14. Available at http://globalbrief.ca/blog/category//features, accessed June 23, 2010.

Sweetman, Arthur. 2003. "Immigrant Source Country Educational Quality and Canadian Labour Market Outcomes." Analytical Studies Research Paper Series, No. 234. Ottawa: Statistics Canada.

Sweetman, Arthur, and Casey Warman. 2009. "Temporary Foreign Workers and Former International Students as a Source of Permanent Immigration." CLSRN Working Paper 25. Canadian Labour Market and Skills Researcher Network.

———. 2010a. "Canada's Temporary Foreign Workers Programs." *Canadian Issues: Temporary Foreign Workers* (Spring), pp. 19–24.

———. 2010b. "A New Source of Immigration: The Canadian Experience Class." *Policy Options* 31 (7): 58–61.

Thompson, Eden, and Christopher Worswick. 2005. "Canadian Research on Immigration and the Labour Market: An Overview." Unpublished.

Timlin, Mabel F. 1951. *Does Canada Need More People?* Toronto: Oxford University Press.

Vaillancourt, François. 1980. "Differences in Earnings by Language Group in Quebec, 1970: An Economic Analysis." Quebec City: International Centre for Research on Bilingualism.

Wanner, Richard A. 2003. "Entry Class and the Earnings Attainment of Immigrants to Canada, 1980-1995." *Canadian Public Policy* 29(1): 53-71.

Wanner, Richard A. 2006. "The Effect of Immigration on Non-immigrant Wage Levels and Immigrant-Non-immigrant Wage Differences in Canadian Metropolitan Labour Markets." Unpublished.

Warman, Casey. 2007a. "You Can Take It with You! The Returns to Foreign Human Capital of Male Temporary Foreign Workers." Working Paper 1125. Kingston, ON: Queen's University, Economics Department.

———. 2007b. "Ethnic Enclaves and Immigrant Earnings Growth." *Canadian Journal of Economics* 40 (2): 401–22.

———. 2010. "The Portability of Human Capital of Male Temporary Foreign Workers: You Can Bring It With You." In *Canadian Immigration: Economic Evidence for a Dynamic Policy Environment*, edited by Ted McDonald, Elizabeth Ruddick, Arthur Sweetman, and Christopher Worswick. Kingston, ON: McGill-Queen's University Press.

Warman, Casey, and Christopher Worswick. 2004. "Immigrant Earnings Performance in Canadian Cities: 1981 Through 2001." *Canadian Journal of Urban Research*. 13 (1): 62 – 84.

Weiner, Nan. 2008. "Breaking Down Barriers to Labour Market Integration of Newcomers in Toronto." *IRPP Choices* 14 (September).

Wente, Margaret. 2010. "Politics of population: a few frank words about immigration." *Globe and Mail*, October 7, p. A21.

World Bank. 2008. *Migration and Remittances Factbook 2008*. Washington, DC.

Worswick, Christopher. 2010. "Temporary Foreign Workers: An Introduction." *Canadian Issues: Temporary Foreign Workers* (Spring), pp. 3–5.

About the Authors

CHARLES BEACH

Charles Beach was born and grew up in Montreal, and received a BAH in economics and political science at McGill University and an MA and PhD in economics at Princeton University. He is now a Professor of Economics at Queen's University where he has taught since 1972. He has worked in the areas of econometrics, income distribution and applied labour market analysis. He was a co-founder of the Canadian Econometrics Study Group, the Canadian Employment Research Forum, and Chair of the Data Liberation Initiative at Statistics Canada. He has supervised a large number of graduate students. He was the Editor of Canadian Public Policy/Analyse de politiques (1995 — 2002) and Director of the John Deutsch Institute at Queen's (2001 — 2009), and is currently a research associate at both the C. D. Howe Institute in Toronto and the Institute for Research on Public Policy in Montreal. He has been a co-initiator of several major data projects with various agencies in Ottawa and has been an advisor to many federal departments. He has published a large number of research and policy papers and has written or edited 16 books including Transition and Structural Change in the North American Labour Market (edited with Michael Abbott and Richard Chaykowski, 1997), Canadian Immigration Policy for the 21st Century (edited with Alan Green and Jeffrey Reitz, 2003), Higher Education in Canada (edited with Robin Boadway and Marvin McInnis, 2005), and Retirement Policy Issues in Canada (edited with Robin Boadway and James MacKinnon, 2009). His current research interests are on Canadian immigration policy and retirement policy and analysis.

CHRISTOPHER WORSWICK

Christopher Worswick is a Professor of Economics at Carleton University. Between 1995 and 1999, he held an academic position in the Department of Economics at the University of Melbourne in Australia. He completed his M.A. and Ph.D. at the University of British Columbia and his B.A. (Honours) at Queen's University. His main area of research is labour economics with a particular focus on the economics of immigration. He has published over 20 academic journal articles, eight refereed book chapters and recently co-edited a book on the economics of immigration. Research topics have included: the earnings, unemployment incidence and benefit receipt of immigrants; the labour supply and educational investments of immigrant married couples; the sensitivity of individual earnings to the macroeconomic conditions; and the school performance and educational outcomes of the children of immigrants. In 2008/2009, he was the Priority Leader for Economic and Labour Market Integration for the Metropolis Network of Research Centres in Canada and in this role was guest editor for a special volume of Canadian Issues/Thèmes Canadiens on Temporary Foreign Workers (published in 2010). He was twice awarded the John Vanderkamp Prize for best article in Canadian Public Policy (1994 with Charles Beach and 1998 with Ted McDonald).

ALAN GREEN

Alan Green died on November 3, 2010 at the age of 78. He was born and raised in Hamilton, Ontario, did his undergraduate work at Queen's University, and carried on to earn a PhD in economics from Harvard University. He taught at Queen's from 1963 until his retirement in 1997, and remained an active teacher and researcher as an emeritus professor well after his retirement. Canadian economic history was his principal forte and he became the dean of economic historians in Canada. He authored or edited 9 books including Regional Aspects of Canada's Economic Growth (1970), Immigration and the Post-war Canadian Economy (1976), and Canadian Immigration Policy for the 21st Century (edited with Charles Beach and Jeffrey Reitz, 2003). He also wrote influential and frequently cited papers on immigration policy, the Great Depression in Canada, regional economic disparities and economic growth, measures of output growth for Canada, and surveys of 20th century Canadian economic history. He was a frequent advisor to the federal government on immigration policy and objectives. He also played the major role in the fund-raising and construction of the Joseph S. Stauffer Library at Queen's University, and in his memory the library's Fireplace Room has been dedicated.

Members of the C.D. Howe Institute

Julien Hutchinson
Richard W. Ivey
Jon R. Johnson
Robert Johnstone
John A. Kazanjian
Kenneth Kelly
Claire M.C. Kennedy
Thomas E. Kierans
James T. Kiernan
David A. Leslie
Henry Lotin
J.W. (Wes) MacAleer
John MacNaughton
Catherine Marsh
R.B. (Biff)Matthews
James W. McCutcheon
James P. McIlroy
Steven McNair
John D. McNeil
Bruce H. Mitchell
William Molson, CA
Gary P. Mooney
Russell J. Morrison
F.W. Orde Morton
John P. Mulvihill
Edward P. Neufeld
James S. Palmer, C.M., AOE, Q.C.
Nick Pantaleo, FCA
Anne Poschmann
Donald S. Reimer
H. Sanford Riley
Philip Robson
W.P. Rosenfeld, Q.C.
Fred P. Rumak
Guylaine Saucier
Brian Shaw
Mary-Anne Sillamaa
Helen K. Sinclair
Andrew Spence
Wayne Steadman
Christopher Sweeney
Henry W. Sykes, QC
Thomas H.B. Symons
Frederick H. Telmer
John D. Tennant
Craig C. Thorburn

Robert J. Turner
Warren Viegas
Alfred G. Wirth
Adam H. Zimmerman
Luke Zygalko

Corporate, Association and Foundation Members

Advocis
AGF Management Limited
Agnico-Eagle Mines Ltd.
Algoma Central Corporation
Alpha Group
Altus Group
AON Consulting
ARC Financial Corp.
Association of Canadian Pension
    Management
Assuris
Astral Media Inc.
ATB Financial
ATCO Ltd. & Canadian Utilities Limited
Balancing Pool
Bank of America Merrill Lynch
Barrick Gold Corporation
Benecaid
Bennett Jones LLP
Blake Cassels & Graydon LLP
BMO Financial Group
BMO Life Assurance Company
Bombardier Inc.
Borden Ladner Gervais LLP
Brookfield Asset Management Inc.
Brookfield Renewable Power
Bruce Power
BURNCO Group of Companies
Business Council of British Columbia
Business Development Bank of Canada
Cadillac Fairview Corp. Ltd.
Caisse de dépôt et placement du Québec
Campbell Strategies
Canada Deposit Insurance Corporation
Canada Overseas Investments Limited
Canadian Association of Petroleum Producers